Virality!

Your Playbook for How to Use AI and Social
Media Marketing to Go Viral and Get Paid

Austin Armstrong

SayThat Publishing LLC

SAY THAT

SayThat Publishing

Contents

Dedication   1

Foreword   3

Introduction   7

PART 1   19

Chapter 1   21
From Myspace Trains to Million-Dollar Lanes

Chapter 2   27
Don't Go Up A Weight Class Before You're Ready

Chapter 3   33
From Unpaid Intern to Industry Leader

Chapter 4   41
How Attending One Conference Changed My Life

Chapter 5   49
Getting Fired Was The Best Thing

Chapter 6   59
From 5K to 100K Subscribers in 3 Days

Chapter 7   65
Creating AI Avatar Videos That Got Millions of Views

Chapter 8 71
From Agency to Startup, The Birth of Syllaby

Chapter 9 81
Becoming An International Speaker

Chapter 10 89
Over 1 million Views With Faceless YouTube Channel

PART 2: Tactical Strategies. It's Go Time. 97

Chapter 11 99
The S.T.A.R.T. Video Framework

Chapter 12 123
Engagement Hacks That Actually Work

Chapter 13: Instagram 135

Chapter 14: Facebook 161

Chapter 15: Threads 185

Chapter 16: TikTok 197

Chapter 17: YouTube 225

Chapter 18: LinkedIn 241

Chapter 19 253
Affiliate marketing

Chapter 20 279
The Future Of What We Sell Online

Chapter 21 283
The Future Of Social Media

Gratitude 289

About Austin Armstrong 291

Connect with Austin 293

Dedication

This book is dedicated to my wife, Austin. My best friend and the love of my life.

You're the person I look forward to being around every single day. We challenge each other, we lift each other up, and together we're building our empire.

I wouldn't be half the man I am without you by my side.

I love you.

Foreword

By Dennis Yu

It's 2:19 AM, and I just finished reading Austin Armstrong's book. I should be asleep, but I couldn't put it down. It felt like Austin was sitting across the table, speaking directly to me.

I know the grind of being a creator. The long nights, the content that flops, the frustration of putting in years of work for what feels like no payoff. Austin has lived that too. For twenty years, he's been figuring it out, learning SEO, testing on YouTube, experimenting on TikTok, building apps and agencies, failing more times than he can count. But in those failures, he found the seeds of success.

Austin and I both admired Gary Vaynerchuk's "hustle harder" mantra. But we also learned the same lesson: hustle without strategy will break you. What changes everything is mentorship, recognizing patterns, and doubling down on what works.

For Austin, that shift happened in 2019 at Video Marketing World. He connected with mentors who taught him how the algorithm really works, the importance of the first three seconds, why research matters, and how to scale winners. Before that, he had uploaded 600 videos in three years and only gained 5,000 subscribers. After applying what he learned, he jumped to 100,000 subscribers in three days. That's not luck, that's leverage.

The same story repeated on TikTok. After endless attempts, one video went viral. Instead of shrugging it off as random, he studied it, replicated it, and built on it. That's the mindset shift: stop chasing everything, and start multiplying what already works.

I've lived this myself. Thousands of my videos have gone nowhere, but every once in a while, one blows up. The difference is whether you call it chance or whether you ask, *Why did this work? How do I make it happen again?*

What I love about Austin is that he doesn't keep this to himself. He could've locked it behind masterminds or high-ticket programs. Instead, he's sharing it openly because he knows there's enough opportunity for all of us.

This book isn't hype. It's not theory. It's raw experience turned into clear principles:

- When you find a winner, 10X it.

- Automate only after you've proven it works.

- Hustle is fuel, but strategy is the steering wheel.

If you read this with focus, you'll find yourself, like me, staring at the clock in the middle of the night, thinking, *This applies to me. I can use this right now.*

Austin didn't write this to get famous. He already has billions of views, multiple seven-figure businesses, and tools like Syllaby that are reshaping how content is made. He wrote it to pay it forward. To shorten your learning curve, to save you years of wasted trial and error.

That's why I'm honored to write this foreword. My hope is that you don't just read, but act. Take these lessons, apply them, and then share your wins with others. Because that's how we all grow.

The book in your hands is going to change how you create. I wish I had it when I started.

Now you do.

Dennis Yu

CEO, BlitzMetricsCo-Author, The Definitive Guide to TikTok Ads

Introduction

Fifteen years of banging my head against the wall.

Would I ever reach the point where the content I poured my life into actually made money?

I studied the greats, Gary Vaynerchuk (a personal favorite and mentor from afar) and others, all preaching the same mantra: "Just keep going. It'll click eventually."

But when?

How many more nights would I stare at my bank account before ordering off a menu, calculating if I could afford what I actually wanted? How many more low-revenue clients would I take on, clients who could barely pay us, who drained more energy than they were worth, just to scrape by on razor-thin margins?

That night, my stomach grumbled as I scanned the menu. My eyes went straight to the prices, not the food. It wasn't about what I craved. It was about what I could afford. Once again, I asked myself: When will I finally be able to order what I want without worrying about the cost?

That night I went home with a semi-full belly... but a heart that was still hungry. Hungry to make all of this *work*.

Just like so many nights before, I fell asleep with the voices of the greats echoing in my head. Gary's words were loudest: **"Just keep going. It'll click at some point."**

But *when?*

I had no idea the answer would be: *the very next morning.*

The alarm blared. After 10 rounds of snoozing, I finally dragged myself out of bed and went straight to the computer. I had my three most important tasks lined up already, because *this* is what trusting the process actually looks like.

The "unsexy" truth of content creation that I had put into practice for 15 years:

- Research

- Writing scripts

- Recording, editing, re-editing

- Designing thumbnails and graphics in Canva

- Prepping for workshops

- Checking analytics on repeat 10 times per day

- Rinse and repeat.

And after all these steps, I would finally feel good enough about a video to upload it to YouTube.

Click. Publish. Let's check email before diving into the next to-do.

I opened my inbox. First two messages: junk. The third one... stopped me in my tracks.

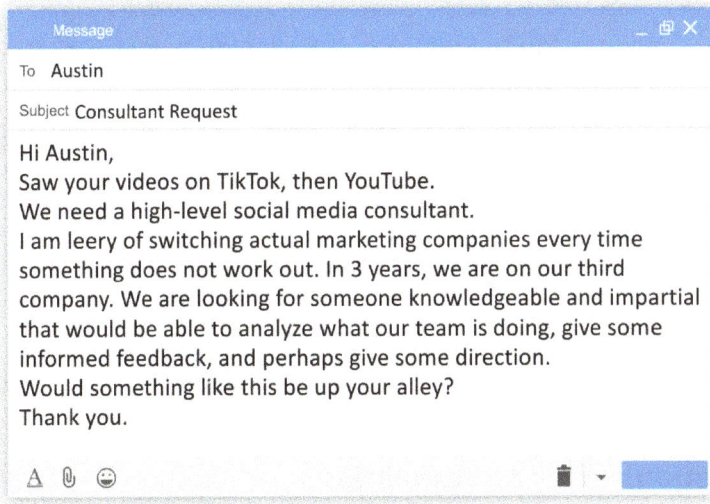

Message	_ ⬜ ✕
To **Austin**	
Subject **Consultant Request**	

Hi Austin,
Saw your videos on TikTok, then YouTube.
We need a high-level social media consultant.
I am leery of switching actual marketing companies every time something does not work out. In 3 years, we are on our third company. We are looking for someone knowledgeable and impartial that would be able to analyze what our team is doing, give some informed feedback, and perhaps give some direction.
Would something like this be up your alley?
Thank you.

A ✂ ☺   🗑 ▾

I blinked.

Me?

I responded. Several conversations later, they asked for a proposal.

I had never pitched a big number before. I held my breath and sent it: **$15,000 for three months.**

They didn't even blink. Contract signed.

I stood up, hands in the air, yelling: **"YEEEEEES!"** Pumping my fists in the air: "YES! YES! YES! YES!"

The elation? Indescribable. That one email, sparked by a single video with only 400 views, **changed everything**.

I'm self-taught. No college degree. But I've got the tenacity of someone who's spent 15 years preparing for this exact moment.

If you take just one thing from this book, let it be this:

Stop thinking like a content creator. Start thinking like an entrepreneur who creates content.

What took me 15 years to figure out, I'm going to teach you in this book.

But fair warning: I'm blunt. I don't have time for your excuses: "I'm too tired." "I'm too busy." "I don't have the right equipment." **Perfectionism is procrastination.**

Some of what I share may make you feel uncomfortable. Good. That's where growth begins.

Everything in this book is based on real-world experience. I've tested these methods across tens of thousands of posts, for myself and for clients in dozens of industries. They've helped me:

- Grow my personal brand to millions of followers.

- Generate billions of organic views.

- Build two multiple 7-figure companies.

- Create multiple 6-figure revenue streams from video and social media.

But I didn't do it alone.

Throughout this book, you'll meet some of the people who helped shape my journey, mentors, business partners, and thought leaders.

And if you go to my website (austinarmstrong.ai/resources), I have a lot of the tips, strategies, and AI tools indexed there for you!

This book is split into **two powerful parts**, each with a distinct purpose:

PART 1: STORIES, GOLDEN NUGGETS & AC-TIONABLE TAKEAWAYS

From the trenches to the top: 20 years of trial, error, and breakthrough.

This first half of the book is where I take you behind the curtain. You'll see the real, raw, and unpolished version of my journey, from being a teenager chasing attention on Myspace... to building multiple multi-million-dollar businesses built on content, community, and consistency.

I'm not giving you the highlight reel. You'll see the messy starts, the risks that didn't pay off, the nights I doubted everything, and the wins that made it all worth it.

Here's the format for every chapter in Part 1:

1. **The Story:** A pivotal, personal moment from my career, told in detail so you can feel it and relate to it.

2. **Golden Nuggets:** The distilled wisdom from that chapter. Quick, high-impact truths you can carry forward.

3. **Actionable Takeaways:** A simple checklist or exercise to help you apply what you just read immediately.

By the end of Part 1, you'll know:

- Why zooming out and focusing on your long-term vision changes everything

- How to turn your biggest failures into competitive advantages

- What no one tells you about shifting from "creator" to "business owner"

- How finding the right mentor can shortcut years of trial and error

- How to keep going when it feels like everything's against you

This section is part motivation, part blueprint, part inner fire. Think of it as the **mindset foundation** for everything you'll build in Part 2.

PART 2: THE TACTICAL STRATEGIES

The tools, systems, and workflows to scale your brand to millions.

If Part 1 is the *why*, this is the *how*. This section is where inspiration meets execution. No fluff, no theories, just the exact strategies I use right now to grow brands, automate content, and turn followers into income streams using social media and AI.

By the end of Part 2, you'll have:

- Psychological triggers to grab attention and keep it

- Step-by-step strategies for TikTok, YouTube, Facebook, Instagram, and more

- My favorite AI tools and automation workflows to save dozens of hours a week

- Ready-to-use content systems you can copy, paste, and customize

- Revenue playbooks for affiliate marketing, micro-SaaS, courses, brand deals, and lead generation

- My predictions for the future of content creation (and how to stay ahead)

Quick Note Before We Dive In: I know the AI space moves fast. The tools and strategies in this book are working right now, but depending on when you read this, the exact platforms or features might have changed. That's okay. The *tactics* will evolve. The *principles* won't: solve real problems, stay adaptable, build your personal brand, and create systems that deliver value. If you lock in those fundamentals, you'll thrive, no matter how the algorithm changes.

Who Am I (and Why Should You Listen to Me)?

If you just stumbled on this book through a post, a video, or maybe it was handed to you by a friend, you might be asking yourself: *"Who is this guy, and why should I listen to him?"*

Fair question. So let me take you back.

I've been playing in the social media game for over 20 years, back when MySpace was the place and Tom was your first friend by default. I was just a teenager, but I had already figured out something most people didn't know yet: **attention is a currency.**

I built hundreds of thousands of followers promoting local bands, t-shirt brands, and even selling custom HTML codes for MySpace profiles. I created my first SaaS product, *GetAdds*, which helped people grow their MySpace presence through automation and viral sharing. I even made money doing email lead generation for digital marketers.

I didn't realize it at the time, but that was my crash course in digital entrepreneurship, learning how to grow an audience, monetize attention, and use technology to make it happen faster.

Fast forward a few years. I moved to California with nothing but a packed car and a lot of uncertainty. I started from the very bottom as an unpaid intern at a video marketing agency in the behavioral health space. I worked my way up, from unpaid intern —> paid intern —> full-time employee —> team leader.

That job taught me the power of content that actually helps people, content that can change lives. Eventually, I launched my own agency, *Socialty Pro*, and worked with hundreds of businesses to grow their brands through organic content, especially video.

Today, I have a combined audience of over 4 million followers across TikTok, Facebook, YouTube, and Instagram. But here's the thing: I didn't get there by chasing trends or doing the latest dance challenge (no shade if that's your thing).

I got there by:

- Staying consistent

- Testing relentlessly

- Studying platforms and algorithms

- Solving real problems through valuable content

I've also built and launched multiple AI software companies, including:

- **Syllaby.io**: An AI-powered content tool for generating scripts, avatars, and videos, then scheduling them across platforms.

- **Bibley.io**: A faith-based AI platform that helps people better understand the Bible.

- **FastRead.io**: An AI book-writing platform for outlining and producing books and audiobooks.

- **FastPhoto.io**: An AI image tool that lets you train on your own headshots and create any image in your likeness.

In addition, I co-founded the "AI Marketing World" Conference, a leading event bringing together marketers, creators, and business owners to explore how AI is changing everything about business, marketing, and creativity.

And in 2025, I had the opportunity to teach "AI entrepreneurship" at Duke University, giving students *real-world* strategies, not theory.

I've built my career by learning what works, putting it into practice, and staying consistent over time. Everything in this book comes from doing, testing, and refining, not from reading a blog post or watching a YouTube video.

This isn't fluff. This isn't clickbait. It's the exact playbook I've used to:

- Grow my audience to millions

- Build multiple 6- and 7-figure revenue streams.

- Leverage AI to produce content at scale.

- Help others do the same.

Whether you're starting from scratch or have been grinding for years without big results, my goal is to give you **the strategies, systems, and mindset you need to build a business, not just a channel.**

PART 1

Chapter 1

From Myspace Trains to Million-Dollar Lanes

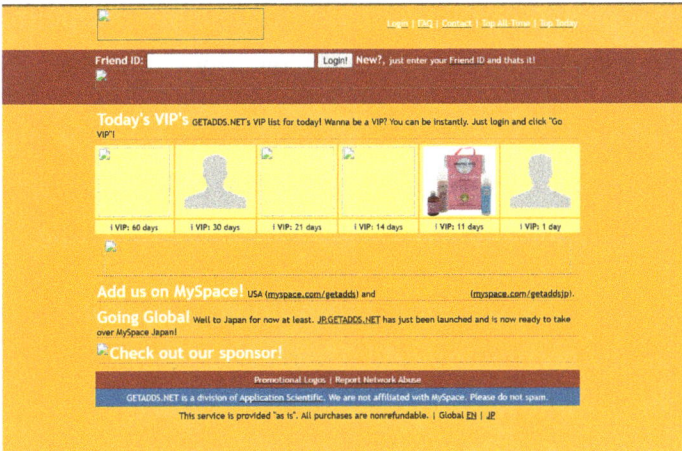

I was 14 years old, sitting in my bedroom with the whine of a dial-up modem filling the air, about to stumble into a world that would change my life forever. And no, I wasn't supposed to be there. Back then, no one was checking IDs to see if you were "old enough" for social media. We were the first generation writing the rules as we went, and breaking most of them.

The platform? Myspace. Any "friends of Tom" reading this?

I didn't know it at the time, but those messy, chaotic days on Myspace would become the foundation for a career I'd still be building two decades later.

At first, I was just curious. But curiosity quickly turned into obsession when I saw people with thousands, even tens of thousands, of friends. *WOW,* I thought. *I want that kind of attention. That recognition.*

If I'm being real, it probably went deeper than that. I grew up in a divorced household, and I carried a lot of anger from it. Maybe part of me was looking for a place where I could matter, where I could be seen and heard. Myspace became my escape from real life, and it gave me a voice I didn't have anywhere else.

School? I hated it. I was a terrible student, constantly in trouble. And if you're an entrepreneur, I bet you're nodding right now. That "don't tell me what to do" gene was already strong.

So, every day after school, I'd rush home, skip homework, and disappear into my online world. There, I found others just like me, early pioneers who lived for growing their profiles. We connected through AOL Instant Messenger (AIM) group chats with over 100 users, all buzzing with ideas, hacks, and HTML code.

Before "collaboration" was even a buzzword, we were doing it daily. We'd drop our profile code into the group chat, copy each other's code, and post it to promote one another. It could take hours, but the results were worth it. We grew together, fast.

And then came the money. I was 15 or 16, making more than I ever thought possible at that age. We promoted bands, t-shirt brands, and even generated leads for early online marketers. But the biggest breakthrough came when my friend Tim, a genius programmer from school, and I built a Myspace SaaS tool called *GetAdds*.

It automated the whole process of promoting profiles, which we called "trains." Join for free and get exposure, or pay for priority placement and get even more friends. In our little world, it was revolutionary.

We had built a system. A business. And then, it all... vanished!

One day, without warning, Myspace deleted our profiles. Years of work, gone in an instant. No warning, no appeal, no conversation. Just a cold reminder that social media is rented space.

That moment hit me hard. Some of us started over. Many quit entirely. I realized then, and would relearn again and again on TikTok, Facebook, and beyond, you cannot build your future on someone else's platform.

After Myspace faded, I lost momentum. Facebook and YouTube were taking over, but I didn't have a mentor telling me to keep going. I drifted for a few years, chasing other paths.

But Myspace had already lit the spark. Even though the platform was gone, the lessons stayed. Those AIM chats, the late nights networking, the rush of building something people wanted, they were the DNA of the entrepreneur I would become.

Today, 20+ years later, the tools have changed, the stakes are higher, it's more competitive, but the mission is clearer than ever.

I still carry that 14-year-old kid inside me. He wasn't just chasing followers. He was chasing freedom.

GOLDEN NUGGETS

Start messy. Start early. You'll never feel "ready." I started with no plan, no skills, just curiosity. Publishing imperfect content is how you build skill, confidence, and momentum.

Collaboration is the ultimate growth hack. From Myspace "trains" to TikTok collabs, teaming up accelerates growth. Share audiences, create together, and lift each other up.

Don't build your house on rented land. Social media platforms can delete you overnight. Own your assets, your email list, website, and text list, so you're never fully at the mercy of someone else's rules.

Automate the repetitive. We built GetAdds to cut hours of manual work. Today, AI can do even more, scripting, editing, posting, analytics, and even now, building those software tools for you. Automate so you can focus on the high-value, creative work only you can do.

ACTIONABLE TAKEAWAYS

Audit your foundation: Make a list of the ways you're driving people *off* social media to something you own (email list, website, text club, or software tool). If the list is short, fix that immediately.

Find your "collab circle": DM 5 creators in your niche this week. Offer something of value and suggest a joint post, live session, or shared project.

Pick one thing to automate: Whether it's scheduling posts, batch-creating scripts, or using AI for captions, commit to saving at least 2 hours a week through automation.

Practice public publishing: Post something *before* you feel ready. Your early content is not your final content, but it will be the bridge to it.

What were your 3 key takeaways:

_____

_____

_____

What 3 additional action steps are you going to take:

_____

_____

_____

What is the deadline you're setting for each of these steps:

_____

_____

_____

Chapter 2

Don't Go Up A Weight Class Before You're Ready

"What are you willing to sacrifice to get the win you want?"

That question burned in my mind after my first Muay Thai fight and my first loss. Yes, before I became known as the AI marketing guy, I was an amateur fighter. I really thought that was going to be my path. I'd already dedicated over a decade of my life to martial arts. I believed fighting was going to be my career. It wasn't. But the lessons I carried from those years? They've shaped everything I've done in business.

It took me four years of training before I finally stepped into the ring. By that point, I was twenty-three, training 2 to 3 hours a day, several days a week. I thought I was in phenomenal shape, and by most people's standards, I was. But fighting isn't just about fitness. It's about timing, sacrifice, and patience.

That's the first lesson: **don't rush the fight.**

Getting into an amateur fight isn't glamorous. You don't get paid. Promoters cancel at the last second. I trained for six different fights before one finally happened. I cut weight, cracked ribs, skipped meals, even skipped Thanksgiving dinner, my favorite holiday, just to stay on point. Each time, the fight fell through.

Frustration set in. I wanted my shot. So when a last-minute fight opened up, I took it. The problem? It was two weight classes higher than I should've been fighting.

Lesson number two: **don't go up a weight class before you're ready.**

At weigh-ins, the difference was brutal. My opponent had cut 20 pounds to make 145. I had to chug water just to barely qualify.

Before the bell rang, standing across from him, it hit me: this guy was a monster. I had signed up to fight a gorilla.

The bell rang anyway. For the next eight minutes, three long rounds, he tossed me around the ring. I didn't get knocked out, but it was a beating.

And yet, I walked out proud. Because I hadn't quit. Because I stood my ground. And because I realized that what looked like a loss was actually a lesson: **you can survive more than you think.**

That fight lit a fire in me.

A few months later, I moved to Atlantic City. The relationship I was in quickly fell apart, and anger became fuel. I found a new gym, ACMMA, and threw myself into training like a man possessed. Mornings started with 3 to 5-mile runs across bridges. Then two-hour sessions. Then back at night for more. Day after day.

That's when I learned the next truth: **discipline beats motivation.** I wasn't motivated every day. But I showed up anyway. And each rep, each run, each drop of sweat stacked in my favor.

When my next fight came, I was ready. This time, I fought at 125, not by accident, but by design. I cut 20+ pounds, lived in saunas, and sucked ice cubes at work because my mouth was so dry. I wanted redemption. I wanted to prove to myself that the sacrifice meant something.

And in the first round, I knocked him out.

That feeling, of sacrifice turning into victory, became the blueprint I carried into business.

Because business, like fighting, is unforgiving. You will take hits. You will face opponents bigger than you. You will want to quit. But if you're willing to sacrifice, if you stay disciplined, if you wait for your weight class and then strike when it's time... you can win.

Whenever I face setbacks now, a failed launch, a client loss, a market collapse, I go back to that ring. I remember the fear, the pain, and the lesson burned into me that night:

Don't step up before you're ready. But when you are ready, step up with everything you've got.

GOLDEN NUGGETS

- **Don't skip levels.** Jumping up two weight classes before I was ready taught me the danger of skipping the fundamentals. Growth is earned through preparation, not shortcuts.

- **Losses sharpen you.** That lopsided loss wasn't a failure. It was fuel. Sometimes defeat is the most honest feedback you'll ever get.

- **Obsession breeds transformation.** I went from "good shape" to elite conditioning when I became obsessed with improvement. Progress requires intensity matched with consistency.

- **Sacrifice fuels the win.** Skipping Thanksgiving dinners, sweating out pounds in saunas, and grinding through exhaustion weren't fun, but they gave me the edge when it mattered.

- **Courage compounds.** If I could stand toe-to-toe with someone trying to hurt me, every business challenge afterward felt smaller by comparison. Facing fear head-on builds unshakable confidence.

ACTIONABLE TAKEAWAYS

1. **Train at your level before moving up.** Don't chase shiny objects or jump into advanced plays before you've mastered the basics. Nail your craft where you are, then scale.

2. **Turn losses into feedback loops.** Write down the 3 biggest lessons from your last "loss" in business (failed campaign, botched launch, missed client). Then create a specific adjustment plan for each.

3. **Commit to intensity + consistency.** Obsession gets results. Set a 30-day "training camp" in your business: choose one skill (sales, video, copywriting) and practice daily, no excuses.

4. **Ask the fighter's question.** "What am I willing to sacrifice to win?" Be honest. Maybe it's sleep, comfort, or Netflix. Name it. Trade it. Growth always costs something.

5. **Reframe fear.** Next time you hesitate on a sales call,

posting a video, or launching an offer, remind yourself: *If I can face down an opponent in the ring, this challenge is nothing.* Anchor back to your courage.

What were your 3 key takeaways:

What 3 additional action steps are you going to take:

What is the deadline you're setting for each of these steps:

Chapter 3

From Unpaid Intern to Industry Leader

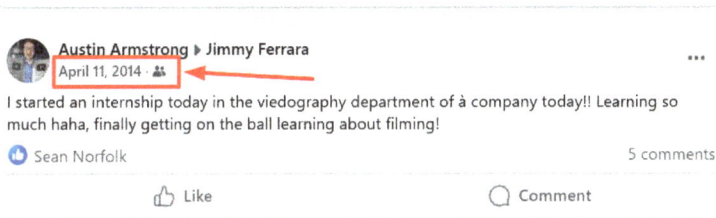

January 2013, just a few months after my last fight. Two friends and I were crammed into my tiny car, everything I owned stuffed into the backseat, barreling down the highway from New Jersey to California.

On the surface, it looked like an adventure. Inside, I was running.

My girlfriend and I had just broken up, my home life had collapsed, and I was staring at a big empty question mark: *What the hell do I want to do with my life?*

I didn't have the answer, but I had an idea, maybe a bold, maybe a reckless one. Start over. Completely.

California gave me three gifts I couldn't have imagined at the time: I met my future wife. I found my calling in video marketing, and I met the mentor who would change the entire trajectory of my life. A few months after I arrived, I stumbled into an internship at the video production and marketing agency, Therapy Cable, that specialized in the behavioral health industry. "Internship" is a generous word. It was unpaid.

And I get it, unpaid internships get a bad rap, especially now. But I've always been a long-term thinker. I didn't see "free labor." I saw *access*. I saw an opportunity. I saw a doorway to somewhere I wanted to go, even if I didn't know exactly where that was yet.

From the first week, something clicked. This was more than marketing. We were helping therapists, psychologists, and addiction specialists put life-saving knowledge on camera, knowledge that could reach the right person at the right time and literally save a life. I remember the first time a client told us, "Someone saw my video and got help before it was too late." That hit different. I was hooked.

I've always shown up hungry. Competition fuels me.

Even at my very first job, a grocery store, I treated it like the Olympics. Every week, the store held competitions for who could scan the most items. The prize? A $5 gift card. Not life-changing money. But for me, it wasn't about the prize. It was about being number ONE. And I was. Week after week. Why? Because I was probably the only one who actually cared.

That same drive carried into my professional career. When I landed my first internship at a marketing agency, I approached it with that same hunger. Within months, I went from unpaid intern —> paid intern —> part-time employee —> full-time employee —> eventually running the agency's operations.

But this climb wasn't without some brutal failures along the way.

One of the most painful (and hilarious, looking back) was when I landed the opportunity to film and interview the team behind an Oscar-nominated short film.

Now imagine: you're only a few months into video production. Do you accept the job? Or do you play it safe and decline?

Of course, I said yes. And I failed **epically.**

Here's what I showed up with:

One camera

One camera battery

One handheld Tascam microphone

One tripod

Six people from the film crew showed up ready to be interviewed.

And what happened was nothing short of a disaster.

The camera battery died constantly, so we had to stop filming for 45 minutes at a time just to charge it. The audio was horrible because no one was mic'd up. By the end of the day, all the footage was completely unusable. I had wasted everyone's time.

And the kicker? That film actually **won the Oscar for Best Short Film.**

Yeah. Ouch.

I was crushed. Embarrassed. Ashamed. But I also made myself a promise: I would *never* show up that unprepared again. That failure lit a fire under me. Instead of breaking me, it sharpened me.

And thankfully, it didn't cost me my job.

Why? Because of my boss, and eventual mentor, Dr. G.

Dr. G wasn't just another agency owner. He was a clinical psychologist, a serial entrepreneur, and one of the sharpest business minds I've ever met. He didn't just hand me tasks; he handed me trust. He saw something in me before I fully saw it in myself.

And he invested in me like no one else ever had. He paid to send me across the country to marketing conferences, sales bootcamps, and one-on-one consulting sessions. Every plane ticket, hotel room, and seminar seat was money out of his pocket, but an investment in my growth.

And I wasn't about to waste it.

That mix of hunger, failure, and mentorship became the foundation of my career.

I was front row at every session, scribbling notes like my life depended on it. I learned that the people who sit up front and ask questions are the ones who leave with the real breakthroughs.

When the agency hit rough waters and eventually failed, Dr. G and I had a choice: walk away or build something new. I pitched him on a traditional agency model. The company before was a different model, which was essentially a revenue-sharing model, where we charged a very low amount to the client to record the content, which means that we actually owned all of the content. And we split the ad revenue from advertisers on top of that. This model, obviously, did not work. For this new agency model, I wanted to be 50/50 partners. He had the money, the experience, the reputation. It seemed only fair.

He shook his head. "You're going to lead this. You should have majority ownership."

That moment is still burned into me. It wasn't just mentorship anymore. This was belief in action.

We called it Socialty Pro. From day one, I made a decision: no cold calling, no "dial until you die" grind. My sales trainers used to tell me to eat an M&M after every cold call as a reward. (Yes, that was a real thing. No, I'm not kidding.) That might work for some, but I wanted to build differently. I'd sometimes stare at the phone, frozen, because I *just* hated cold calling so much. So I had to figure out inbound marketing.

I told myself I would master inbound marketing. I'd earn attention by giving value first.

If you're looking for a social media agency, who do you hire? The one with no followers, or the one with hundreds of thousands, teaching the exact strategies they'll use for you?

It's like picking a personal trainer. You're not hiring the out-of-shape guy who "knows the theory." You're hiring the one who's fit, disciplined, and living it every day.

That philosophy became our edge. Socialty Pro didn't just talk about marketing, we *were* the case study. Our growth was proof that our strategies worked.

And it all started because one mentor poured belief, time, and resources into me.

Not everyone gets a Dr. G. But you can find your version. Sometimes you pay for it. Sometimes you earn it. Sometimes it's a community, a course, or a coach.

But one thing's for sure: **You are your greatest asset. The right mentor will help you see it and own it. Don't be afraid to invest in yourself.**

GOLDEN NUGGETS

Hunger beats talent. I wasn't the most experienced or the most connected, but I showed up hungry. That drive took me from an unpaid intern to running operations. Hunger is a skill in itself. And showing initiative can pay off.

Fail forward My Oscar fail could've ended me, but instead it became fuel. Your worst mistakes often contain your best lessons if you keep moving.

The right mentor changes everything Dr. G didn't just give me tasks; he gave me trust, investment, and eventually ownership. A single mentor can collapse your learning curve by years.

Proof is the best pitch Socialty Pro didn't rely on cold calls. We became our own case study. When people saw our strategies work for us, they trusted us to make them work for them.

ACTIONABLE TAKEAWAYS

1. **Audit your hunger.** Where in your life are you coasting? Pick one area where you can compete with yourself to level up this month.

2. **Redefine failure.** Write down your top 3 "embarrassing" professional mistakes. Next to each, jot the lesson you learned. If you can extract the gold, the failure pays for itself.

3. **Find your Dr. G.** Make a list of 5 people in your industry you'd love to learn from. Reach out with one specific ask and one thing you can offer back (yes, even if it's just energy, support, or referrals). And don't forget that the power is in the follow-up.

4. **Be your own proof.** If you sell marketing, do it for yourself. If you sell fitness, show it in your life. Identify one way

this week to live out the results you promise others.

5. **Claim ownership.** Don't wait for someone to give you a title. Act like the leader now. Write down what "majority ownership" of your life or career would look like and start taking one step toward it today.

What were your 3 key takeaways:

What 3 additional action steps are you going to take:

What is the deadline you're setting for each of these steps:

Chapter 4

How Attending One Conference Changed My Life

When I worked at the video marketing agency, Therapy Cable, Dr. G valued one thing above almost anything else: *keep learning*.

He knew I was obsessed with studying the best in the industry, not just watching their videos, but dissecting how they used marketing to create results. I'd been to a few conferences before, but one in particular kept catching my eye: Video Marketing World.

It felt like it was built for me. I didn't just *do* video marketing. I *was* a video marketer. This conference spoke directly to that identity.

Still, asking to go was a stretch. Earlier that year, we'd gone to VidSummit in Los Angeles, less than an hour from our office in Orange County. But Dallas, Texas? That meant ticket, flight, hotel, meals, everything.

I remember sitting at my desk, rehearsing my pitch in my head like I was about to go into a high-stakes negotiation. I pictured the best-case scenario, imagined myself in the room, learning things that could change everything.

Then I just... asked. "You miss 100% of the shots you don't take," right?

To my surprise, and after a little back and forth to make sure the opportunity was worth it, he said yes. I think Gary Vaynerchuk had something to do with it. At VidSummit, we saw Gary live for the first time. He'd looked out at the crowd, pulled his phone from his pocket, and said:

"This device is where everyone is spending all of their time. Don't wait. Stop making excuses. This is your opportunity. Don't regret not taking action."

That line became a soundtrack in my head.

So in 2019, I flew to Dallas. I didn't know a single person in the room. I sat in the back, notebook open, scribbling furiously through every session, storytelling, retention, frameworks, and monetization. I wasn't just watching speakers. I was *studying* them.

That same year, after the conference, I started posting on TikTok. No one in marketing was paying much attention to it yet. Then the pandemic hit. The world changed. TikTok exploded. And because of what I'd learned, I was ready. Clients came in. Leads came in. My agency grew. I'll teach exactly what I did to get clients on TikTok in the second half of this book.

Two years later, in 2021, I took a shot. I sent a cold DM to Scott Simson, the owner of Video Marketing World. I told him how attending in 2019 had changed my career, and I mentioned something that intrigued him: VMW had never had a TikTok speaker. By then, I had 50,000 followers and a portfolio of real business results from the platform.

He invited me on his podcast. We had a great conversation.

When it ended, I decided not to leave the moment on the table. "One of my dreams is to speak on stage," I told him. "If you ever need someone to cover TikTok, I'd love the opportunity."

Fate? Luck? Timing? Whatever it was, one of his TikTok speakers had just dropped out. I was in.

I moderated the first-ever TikTok for Business panel at VMW 2021. This time, I sat in the front row with new friends. It felt like a *ceremonial promotion* to the front of the room.

The panel went great. But the real shock came at the end of the event when Scott called me to the stage to present me with the "Dark Horse Society" award for generating over $250,000 through video marketing. I knew I was in the running for the award, but didn't expect to receive it.

The panel was so well-received that the following year, I was invited back, this time as a keynote speaker. My first major stage. My first time carrying the full weight of an audience's attention for an entire session. I still remember how nervous I was right before I went out on that stage. I did jumping jacks behind the curtain, shaking out my nerves. And before I knew it, they were announcing my name to walk out as the next speaker. I couldn't back out now...I delivered. And that year, they also gave me the "Gold Dark Horse" award for earning $1 million in revenue from video marketing.

From the back row to the main stage.

Over time, Scott and I became not just collaborators but friends. We shared strategies, hired each other for coaching, and eventually became business partners. Today, we've rebranded Video Marketing World into "AI Marketing World", a conference built for where content creation is heading.

None of it would have happened if I hadn't asked to go to that first conference. If I hadn't cold-messaged Scott. If I hadn't said the words, "I want to speak."

Thinking like a business owner means you stop waiting for the perfect moment. You show up like it matters. You take the shot, again and again, until the opportunities compound.

That's how you build a business, not just a channel.

GOLDEN NUGGETS

One room can change your life. That first conference created a domino effect that changed my career. Proximity to the right people opens doors you can't see yet. That's why I co-founded "AI Marketing World", to create *that room* for others.

Become a student of the game. Don't just network, nurture. I filled notebooks because I knew success leaves clues. Study the best. Reverse engineer their strategies. Apply fast, adjust faster. One DM led to a podcast —> panel —> keynote —> partnership. Meet people, add value, follow up, and keep showing up.

Leverage your wins. A small panel turned into a keynote. A keynote turned into a rebrand and partnership. Stack your wins. From the back row to the stage wasn't overnight. It was the result of relentless, consistent action.

Think like a business owner, not a creator. Shoot your shot. Content is a tool. The goal is building something that lasts beyond any platform or algorithm change. The biggest leaps in my career came from one ask. Don't wait for permission.

ACTIONABLE TAKEAWAYS

Get in the right rooms, even if it's a stretch. Look for one event this year (it should be "AI Marketing World") that directly aligns with your niche or audience. Budget for it now. Treat it like an investment, not an expense.

Prepare before you arrive. Research the speakers, topics, and attendees in advance. Follow them on social media. Comment on their posts before the event so your face (and name) are familiar when you meet in person.

Take notes like you're going to teach them. This forces you to actively process the information instead of passively listening. Then, actually *share* a takeaway from each session on your social platforms within 24 hours. This builds authority immediately.

Follow up fast. Within 48 hours of meeting someone, send a quick message:

- Thank them for their time.

- Mention something specific from your conversation.

- Offer value (a resource, connection, or insight).

Make one bold ask. Turn one win into many. Whether it's speaking on stage, collaborating on a project, or doing a joint livestream, make one specific request before the event energy fades. Post about your conference experience. Tag speakers and the event itself. Share what you learned, what you did differently after, and what results it created. This visibility often leads to your *next* opportunity.

What were your 3 key takeaways:

_____

_____

_____

What 3 additional action steps are you going to take:

_____

_____

_____

What is the deadline you're setting for each of these steps:

_____

_____

_____

Chapter 5

Getting Fired Was The Best Thing

Austin Armstrong ✓
Jul 3, 2020 · 🌐

For the first time in my life I am 100% self employed! This is an exciting and scary experience! If you need any marketing help at all or want to grow your business online, please reach out! I've been doing this for over 15 years and would love to help you dominate online!

See insights and ads   **Boost post**

👍❤️ 97   26 comments 2 shares

One of the best things that ever happened in my career came disguised as a gut punch: I got fired, two months into the COVID pandemic, June 2020. Less than a year after I had gone to my first Video Marketing World (VMW) conference.

At the time, I had moved back across the country from California to North Carolina to support my wife as she pursued her MBA at Duke University. (Yes, that means I'm officially a Blue Devil fan. Suck it, Tar Heels!) It was the first time I had ever gone fully remote for work, which, ironically, I absolutely loved.

I found out I was going to be fired in the dumbest way imaginable.

I was CC'ed, accidentally or maybe not, on an internal email thread between a few executives and the marketing team. The message was clear: they were planning to let me go. I read it, stunned.

Am I reading this right? I thought. *They're firing me? I've been delivering results. I'm deeply integrated into everything. How could this be happening?*

Then the call came. They gave me some vague, passive-aggressive excuse about "self-promotion" being too excessive. It was BS. And just like that, I was done.

Fired. In the middle of a global pandemic. With no college degree and no clear next step.

I was angry. I was hurt. I was worried.

But I also had a choice.

I sat down separately with my wife and my longtime mentor and business partner, Dr. G. Thankfully, I had already started a small side hustle, a marketing agency called Socialty Pro. I also had three months of savings. That was it.

So I stood at the classic entrepreneurial fork in the road: Do I try to find another job in the middle of a pandemic... or do I bet on myself?

With full support from my wife and Dr. G, I chose to go all in. I bet on myself.

And it worked.

After going full-time into Socialty Pro, I made another bold decision: I went all in on TikTok.

I'd been a fan of Gary Vaynerchuk for years, and he had been screaming about TikTok nonstop. I figured, "Alright, alright, I'll give it a real shot." So I started creating. And guess what happened?

Absolutely nothing.

My videos flopped. I had no traction. Zero growth. I was trying trends, mixing in some business content, and even did the cringe-worthy follow-for-follow (don't do that, it's a complete waste of time). Three months in, I was spinning my wheels.

Then I saw a Facebook ad that changed everything. It was a free webinar by a marketer named Rachel Pedersen called *"TikTok for Business."* I wasn't doing anything else that day, so I figured, "Why not?"

What happened during that webinar was one of those rare light-bulb moments. Rachel broke down advanced TikTok strategies, like how to use long-tail keyword questions, niche hashtags, and evergreen lead-gen content. She showed case study after case study of businesses using simple Q&A videos to attract customers.

And that's when it clicked for me.

As someone who had studied SEO and YouTube optimization for years, I immediately saw how her strategies could translate directly into what I already knew how to do. These creators weren't dancing. They were teaching. They were building businesses. They were solving problems.

That was the shift.

I decided right then: I'm going to create only business content, every single day, for 30 days straight. If I get zero traction, I'll move on.

But something happens when you commit with clarity and urgency. Magic happens.

By day 14, I started to see growth. Comments. Shares. Followers.

And more importantly: leads. Real business inquiries coming in from my TikTok videos.

I experimented with different types of marketing content, LinkedIn tips, video strategy, Pinterest hacks, and helpful websites for entrepreneurs. But then I posted one video that changed everything.

It was a simple tutorial on how to reduce image file size and add ALT text before uploading it to your website. Super niche. Kind of boring.

It got over 1 million views.

That's when the real growth began.

The comments poured in, hundreds of them. People were asking follow-up questions, wanting deeper advice, and requesting related content. So I did something strategic: I responded to as many comments as I could using TikTok's video reply feature.

This created a chain reaction. Each video reply linked back to the original viral video. I made 40 or 50 responses this way, all feeding engagement to the video that started it all. That feature is one of TikTok's secret growth weapons, and I used it relentlessly.

Within a few months, I grew to 50,000 followers. But more than that, I had proof of concept.

TikTok, a platform most people still dismissed, was generating leads, building authority, and fueling real income. It wasn't just social media anymore. It was a business channel.

That moment of being fired, the panic, the doubt, the anger, led me to this. A new chapter. A new business model. A new platform that would change the entire trajectory of my career.

And funny enough, that webinar host? Rachel Pedersen? We're now good friends. I even had her on my podcast, *BusinessTok.* She's brilliant, kind, and a massive part of why I found success on TikTok. I've told her, personally, how much her teaching impacted me. That's the power of sharing what you know. You never know who's listening.

The more experienced I became in business, the more lessons I learned, like the importance of increasing your pricing. Those razor-thin margin clients I mentioned earlier? Yeah, they're actually more needy because they can barely afford you in the first place. Believe it or not, the more you charge people, the easier the work becomes in most cases.

There's just a big shift in the mindset of a solopreneur barely scraping by, and the more established business owner who has more budget to allocate. They just don't look at money the same way. The solopreneur, in my experience, makes slower buying decisions and nitpicks everything. The more experienced business owner moves fast, studies the results, and then continues to move fast.

This results in a much better working situation. Personally, I found that increasing my prices by 3-4x actually resulted in: A) Less client headache. B) More freedom to be treated as an expert without micro-managing. C) More profit for our business.

So ask yourself: if you're charging too little, are your clients a headache? By simply doubling your prices, you can make more money and oftentimes do less work. Assuming your quality is excellent.

So if you're in a moment of uncertainty, let me tell you this: Sometimes, the thing that feels like a setback is actually the setup. Sometimes, getting fired is the beginning of finally being free.And sometimes, the platform you're ignoring is the one that could change your life.

Give it a chance. Bet on yourself. Go all in.

GOLDEN NUGGETS

Your worst day can be your turning point. Getting fired felt like a punch to the gut. But looking back, it was the shove I needed to finally go all in. Sometimes the thing that feels like the end is just the setup for your next chapter.

Bet on yourself when it matters most. I had a choice: play it safe or take the leap. I had three months of savings, a vision, and a supportive wife and mentor. So I bet on myself. The biggest risk? Staying stuck.

Consistency unlocks compound growth. I committed to 30 days of daily TikTok videos about business. Not everything hit, but by day 14, the momentum kicked in. Perfection isn't the goal. Showing up is. One post can change everything.

Find your mentor shortcut. Rachel Pedersen's free TikTok webinar flipped a switch for me. It connected my SEO and YouTube knowledge to TikTok growth. Never underestimate the power of learning from someone who's already built what you're building.

Double down on what clicks. That video on reducing image file size? One million views. I turned it into a series by replying to hundreds of comments with follow-up videos. That created a viral loop and drove massive reach. When something works, don't move on, go deeper.

ACTIONABLE TAKEAWAYS

Write your own "setback story." Journal about the last time something felt like the end but actually pushed you toward growth. This will reframe how you view challenges.

Pick one platform and go all in for 30 days. Daily posts. No excuses. At the end, review your analytics and decide what worked.

Experiment with comment replies. Turn your comment section into a content engine. Respond to at least 10 comments per week with new videos.

Audit your pricing. If you've been stuck with low-paying, high-maintenance clients, consider doubling your rates for new clients. Test the results.

Find one mentor shortcut. Sign up for a free webinar, follow an expert's content, or read their book. Compress time by standing on their shoulders. For instance, I have tons of free resources for you at .

What were your 3 key takeaways:

_____

_____

_____

What 3 additional action steps are you going to take:

_____

_____

_____

What is the deadline you're setting for each of these steps:

_____

_____

_____

Chapter 6

From 5K to 100K Subscribers in 3 Days

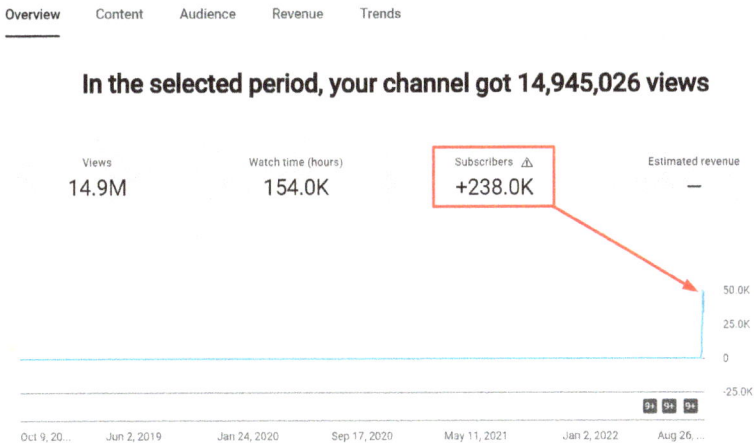

One of the most surreal moments of my entire content journey happened while I was sitting on a beach in Tulum, Mexico, sipping a Mezcalita and casually checking YouTube Studio... as my channel exploded in real time.

But that's not where the story starts.

At this point, I had been grinding for three years to grow my personal brand on YouTube. TikTok? I had traction, millions of views, real leads, and paying clients. But YouTube? That platform felt like a puzzle I couldn't solve.

It wasn't for lack of effort. I had posted over 600 videos, mostly Shorts, with some long-form mixed in. I was consistent, I tested, I studied. But after all that, my channel had barely cracked 5,000 subscribers.

Now, for some, that's progress. But I'm not wired for "decent." I wanted real impact.

That's when my friend, one of the top YouTube strategists in the world, stepped in.

Jeremy Vest has helped brands like VidIQ, Braille Skateboarding, and Zapier reach millions of subscribers and billions of views. He doesn't play small, and he doesn't guess. So when he said, *"Let's figure this out together,"* I was all in.

For the next few weeks, we jumped on daily Zoom calls. We dissected the DNA of top-performing channels:

- The exact structure of viral videos

- How to title Shorts for maximum curiosity

- The importance of the first three seconds

- Hook stacking, scene pacing, and loopable endings

- And, most importantly, upload strategy

That last one was the game-changer.

Up until then, I had been dumping every TikTok video straight onto YouTube. No filtering, no prioritizing, just post-and-pray. Jeremy's advice? Stop. Only post your *best* performers.

At the time, I had a TikTok series called *"These 5 Websites Feel Illegal to Know."* It had tens of millions of views. It was curiosity-driven, practical, and insanely shareable. So I decided to go all in.

For one week, I posted nothing but those videos, two to three per day.

Then, it happened.

The YouTube algorithm grabbed them and ran.

In three years, I had crawled from zero to 5,000 subscribers. In the next **three days**, I skyrocketed to over **100,000**.

Back in Tulum, I kept refreshing YouTube Studio on my phone like a madman. *"Austin, look!"* I told my wife. (Yes, fun fact, her name is also Austin.) *"I'm getting hundreds of thousands of views per hour!"*

She smirked, took a sip of her drink, and said, *"Cool. But we're in Mexico. Put your f*#$in' phone down."*

And she was right.

That moment reminded me of something important: It's not just about the numbers. It's about what those numbers make possible.

Freedom. Flexibility. The ability to sit across from someone you love, on a beach, and know you built a life where this is normal.

That spike in subscribers wasn't just a professional breakthrough. It was a personal one.

Create like a Business Owner. Scale like a strategist. But live like you've already made it.

Because if you're not enjoying the life you're building, what's the point?

GOLDEN NUGGETS

Effort without strategy = burnout 600 videos in 3 years for 5K subs wasn't a lack of effort, it was a lack of direction.

Mentors speed up success: Jeremy didn't just give tips; he gave me a map.

Double down on winners: The "Illegal Websites" series wasn't a fluke; it was leverage.

Tiny pivots create massive results: One small shift, posting only my best TikToks to YouTube, changed everything.

Remember your "why": Tulum wasn't about the Wi-Fi speed; it was about the life I had built to be there.

ACTIONABLE TAKEAWAYS

Audit your content library. Identify the top 5-10% of posts that performed best on any platform.

Repurpose with intention. Don't dump content everywhere; strategize how you will tailor your uploads to each platform's audience and algorithm.

Focus on your hook. Spend extra time perfecting the first 3 seconds of your video.

Set a "life checkpoint." Every quarter, step back and ask: "Am I enjoying the life I'm building?"

What were your 3 key takeaways:

_____

_____

_____

What 3 additional action steps are you going to take:

_____

_____

_____

What is the deadline you're setting for each of these steps:

_____

_____

_____

Chapter 7

Creating AI Avatar Videos That Got Millions of Views

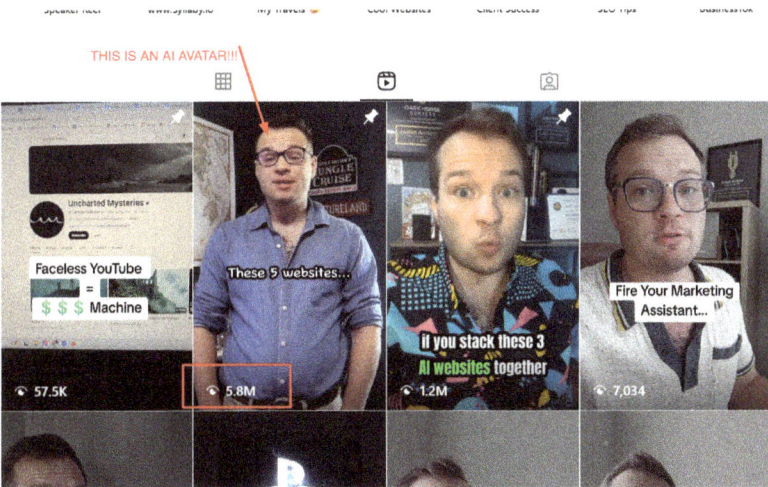

The first time I saw an AI avatar video, I got excited by the possibilities.

Soon after, when I made my first AI avatar, on the screen was someone who looked exactly like me, but wasn't me. Same face, same voice, same little head tilt, I didn't even know I did. It was eerie, unsettling... and electrifying.

If you've never seen an AI avatar before, here's the gist: you record yourself once, and the system clones you. From then on, you never need to press record again. You just type a script, hit generate, and boom, there you are on screen, talking as if you filmed it live.

One recording. Infinite reuse. Content on demand.

When Synthesia started popping off on TikTok, I was hooked. Their channel, @synthesia.ai, was going viral with proof-of-concept clips, and I couldn't look away. This was the exact future I had imagined when I founded Syllaby.

Then HeyGen hit the market, and things leveled up. Their avatars weren't just functional. They were *good*. Too good. Affordable, easy, and so realistic it was almost scary.

At that point, Syllaby didn't have its own avatar tech yet, so I did what every scrappy entrepreneur does: I borrowed someone else's. I grabbed HeyGen's enterprise deal and thought: *Let's see how far this can really go.*

And I didn't just dabble. I went mad scientist.

I designed four different avatars of myself and launched one of the largest case studies I've ever done: over **1,000 AI avatar videos** across four niches.

- Real Estate

- Mental Health & Addiction Recovery

- Investing

- Re-creations of my own top-performing content

For weeks, I pumped out videos, tracked numbers, and waited.

The results? A mixed bag.

Real estate and investing content? Dead on arrival. Zero tractio n.Mental health and addiction recovery? Surprisingly strong, tens of thousands of views. But the real game-changer was re-creating my *own* best hits.

That's when the algorithm went wild.

I took videos I had already recorded in the past, fed the exact scripts into my AI avatar, and regenerated them word-for-word. And here's the kicker: some of those AI clones *outperformed the originals.*

One of them, me in a simple blue shirt, has now been reposted multiple times, racking up **over 5 million views** on Instagram alone. You can still find it pinned on my profile @socialtypro.

Let me put that in perspective: the *fake* version of me was pulling in more attention than the real me.

That blew my mind.

But then came the real test. The "mom test."

One sunny afternoon in Southern California, I was sitting across from my mom at lunch. We were outside, birds chirping, plates clinking, sunlight bouncing off the table. I decided to show her one of my new AI avatar videos, curious to see if she'd catch on.

She watched for a few seconds, squinted, then looked up at me and said, softly:

"Oh, honey... I don't like this."

Not angry. Not confused. Just disappointed. Which, if you've had a mom like mine, you know, stings worse than anything.

I laughed and admitted it wasn't me, it was AI. She shook her head and said, *"It just doesn't feel like you."*

That stuck with me. Because she was right. AI avatars are powerful, but they can't replace the spark of authenticity that comes through in a real human moment.

And yet, the potential is undeniable.

We're still in the early days, but this technology is already rewriting the rules of how we create, scale, and monetize content. From organic social media and courses to training materials and even cold outreach, AI avatars are opening doors that creators never thought possible.

Some people will reject it. Some will fear it. But the ones who embrace it? They'll shape the future.

GOLDEN NUGGETS

Be curious enough to test what's next. When Synthesia and HeyGen started making noise, I didn't sit on the sidelines. I jumped in. Early adopters often win because they experiment fast.

Leverage tools before you build your own. Buy vs Build. Before Syllaby had avatars, I used HeyGen's enterprise plan to validate the idea. Don't wait for perfection; use what's already available to prove your concept.

Let the data lead, not your ego. Some niches flopped. Others thrived. I didn't take failure personally; I took it as feedback. Data decides where you double down.

Repurposing can outperform originals. My AI-generated re-creations sometimes beat my real videos. When a message is proven, scaling it in new formats creates repeatable wins.

Don't fight the future, create with it. AI is already here. The creators who adapt and build with it will outlast the ones who resist.

ACTIONABLE TAKEAWAYS

Run a mini case study. Pick three niches or themes and test AI avatar videos across them. Let the numbers, not your assumptions, guide your next move.

Re-create one of your best performers. Take a video that already went viral (or performed above average), script it word-for-word, and remake it with an avatar. Compare results.

Audit your toolbox. List the AI tools available now that could accelerate your process. Ask: "Am I waiting to build from scratch when I could be validating today?"

Do the "mom test." your AI avatar video to someone who knows you well. Ask them how it makes them feel. The feedback may surprise you, and sharpen how you use avatars.

Increase your "future bets." Pick one AI-driven experiment per month. Commit to testing, not mastering, what's new. The creators who stack these early bets will ride the next wave first.

What were your 3 key takeaways:

What 3 additional action steps are you going to take:

What is the deadline you're setting for each of these steps:

Chapter 8

From Agency to Startup, The Birth of Syllaby

When I was running my marketing agency, Socialty Pro, I used to say something to my team that probably made them roll their eyes more than once:

"We are not just an agency. We are a proven, repeatable system of growth that just happens to currently be in the life stage of an agency."

At the time, I don't think I fully believed it. But I *wanted* to. Saying it out loud was my way of speaking a future into existence, even if I couldn't yet picture the details. Deep down, though, I knew we weren't meant to stay in an agency forever.

About five years in, the future started to take shape. I caught what I now call *the startup bug.*

At Socialty Pro, I was already creating content about the latest software tools for entrepreneurs and small business owners. Because I was an affiliate for many of those tools, I made solid recurring income, sometimes 20%, even 50% commissions on subscriptions.

But one day, a simple question smacked me in the face:

"Why am I earning 20% promoting someone else's software when I know how to build and sell my own?"

That single thought cracked something open. I gave myself permission to pause and reflect: *What problem do I want to solve? What's the most painful, tedious part of my business right now?*

The answer came fast: **content strategy.**

Onboarding new clients at Socialty Pro meant hours of research, competitor analysis, and building detailed marketing plans. Brutal, time-consuming, and repetitive. *What if I could automate that entire process?*

That was the seed that grew into Syllaby.

I bootstrapped the first version. Hired a team on Upwork. Sank $15,000. Waited six months. And when the minimum viable product (MVP) arrived?

Garbage.

Painful, but powerful lesson: vision doesn't automatically make you the right person to execute every step. I was a marketer, not a technical product manager. And I was out of my depth. Above my weight class, if you will.

But sometimes the wrong path is what leads you to the right people.

That clunky MVP was enough to get me in front of my friend Anand, a technical wizard who instantly *got it.* In a single weekend, he rebuilt what had taken my first team half a year. Cleaner, smarter, and infinitely more functional.

That weekend changed everything.

From there, we refined the product, talked to users, and, crucially, decided to build in public. Most founders operate in "stealth mode," afraid of competition or premature judgment. I believed something different: in marketing, and in life, **people follow stories.**

So I documented it all. The wins, the roadblocks, the redesigns. I invited my audience into the messy middle. And because of that transparency, they didn't just watch, they rooted for us.

When we finally launched, it wasn't with fireworks. It was a one-page landing site with a bold headline, a short pitch, and an early access form. Anyone who signed up got a 50% discount. Simple. Direct. And it worked, applying the principles of a "scarcity mindset" or FOMO (Fear Of Missing Out).

I pushed it hard across my growing social media platforms. Within weeks, we had **10,000 email sign-ups who expressed interest in early access.**

Seven months later, Syllaby was doing **$88,000 in monthly recurring revenue (MRR).**

How? By following a blueprint:

We didn't just launch Syllaby, we built it *with* people, not *for* them.

From day one, we built in public. Every feature, every setback, every redesign was something we shared openly. People weren't just "watching" a startup; they were part of it. And when you invite people into your journey, they don't just buy your product. They root for you to win. That sense of community became one of our strongest growth engines.

But transparency alone doesn't drive traction. You need eyeballs. That's where video came in.

I went all-in on video marketing. Every single day, I pushed out one or two short verticals across TikTok, YouTube, Instagram, and Facebook. On top of that, I dropped one or two long-form YouTube videos every week. It was relentless, but it worked. Consistency creates compounding exposure, and compounding exposure builds trust.

Then we built a home for our early adopters: the *Syllaby Content Creators* Facebook group. What started as a beta group has grown into a thriving community of over **60,000 members.** Inside, we host monthly challenges, share free trainings, bring in guest experts, and most importantly, give people a place to learn and collaborate. It's one of the proudest things I've built, because it's not just about us. It's creators helping creators every single day.

Next came affiliates. As an affiliate marketer myself, I knew the power of an incentive structure that made people want to sell for you. We rolled out a 30% *recurring, lifetime* commission plan and gave affiliates real tools to succeed. The result? Over **11,000 affiliates** signed up. Not all of them were active, but here's the truth: you don't need thousands. You just need a few hundred power affiliates who believe in the mission. That was enough to turn affiliates into an army. (For the curious, we used FirstProm oter.com to manage it all.)

We didn't stop there. We launched on Product Hunt and campaigned hard. That single push won us the coveted **#1 Product of the Day** spot, which sent a flood of traffic and early signups.

Then we went wide. We listed Syllaby across 150+ software directories (you can get this list on the resources page of this book at) from FutureTools and Futurepedia to There's An AI For That. Each one acted like a drip-feed of signups and gave us SEO juice. To boost this further, we also bought ad spots and even sponsored AI and marketing newsletters like *Ben's Bites* and *Superhuman AI.*

And here's one of my favorite growth hacks: influencer partnerships. Instead of blowing our budget on one-off posts, we signed **SAFE note agreements** with influencers. Instead of paying cash, we gave them convertible equity in exchange for promoting Syllaby. The forward-thinking influencers loved it because if their efforts helped increase our valuation, their upside was way bigger than a one-time check. It was a win-win.

Piece by piece, all these moves stacked together. We weren't just launching software, we were building a movement.

Active subscribers ⓘ

1,806

1,806

0

Jan 31, 2023   Aug 31, 2023

View more   Updated 9:45 AM ♦

MRR ⓘ

$88,421.92

$88,421.92

$0.00

Jan 31, 2023   Aug 31, 2023

View more   Updated 9:45 AM ♦

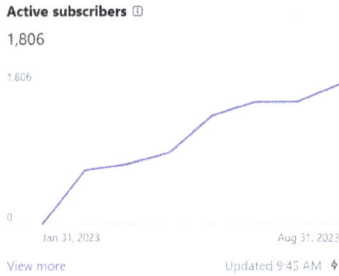

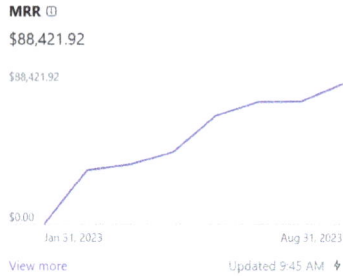

We thought we were on top of the world... until the gut punch landed.

The market shifted overnight. AI avatars, our shiny flagship feature, suddenly flooded the space. Startups were popping up like weeds. The tech wasn't evolving fast enough to match our vision. And worst of all, we were stuck in what I call "AI tourism." Everyone wanted to *try* the shiny new tools, but no one wanted to *stay*. Users were hopping from platform to platform, experimenting, ghosting, moving on. Drastically increasing our churn.

Our momentum evaporated. Revenue nosedived. We watched $88k MRR shrink to just over $40k.

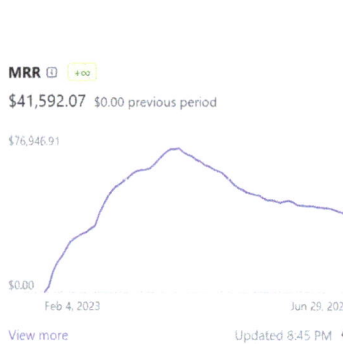

Active subscribers ⓘ +∞

801 0 previous period

1,572

0

Feb 4, 2023   Jun 29, 2024

View more   Updated 8:45 PM ♦

MRR ⓘ +∞

$41,592.07 $0.00 previous period

$76,946.91

$0.00

Feb 4, 2023   Jun 29, 2024

View more   Updated 8:45 PM ♦

It felt like the floor gave out from under us. That could've been the end. Another startup headline about "early promise, sudden fall."

But we weren't done yet.

Instead of panicking, we went back to the source: **our users.** We asked, we listened, we dug into the data. And that's when the real insight clicked:

Avatars were a trend. Faceless content was a need.

Creators weren't begging for clones of themselves. They were begging for a way to post consistently without always being "on." They wanted to create without cameras, without makeup, without budgets. They wanted scale without burnout.

So we made the pivot.

We slashed our price in half to lower the barrier for beginners. We shifted our message from "business owners" to **everyday creators hungry to make money online.** And we rebuilt Syllaby around **faceless video automation.**

Not good. Not decent. Exceptional. Better than anything else in the market.

And this time, it clicked.

Today, Syllaby powers over **2,000 videos a day** for creators all over the world. We rebuilt our revenue to over **$180,000 MRR,** and it's still climbing.

We went from a cold idea to a failed MVP, to a rebuild in a weekend, to a near-collapse, to a $2M+ ARR company.

Not because the path was easy. Not because we never stumbled. But because we believed, we listened, and we dared to pivot, and the willingness to ask ourselves what we were willing to sacrifice to get the win we wanted?

And you know what: **we're still just getting started.**

GOLDEN NUGGETS

Speak your future into existence. Even if you don't fully believe it yet, your words create direction. I called Socialty Pro a "system," not just an agency, before it ever became one.

Solve your own pain first. The seed for Syllaby came from my biggest bottleneck at Socialty Pro: content strategy. Build what you wish existed for yourself.

Fail fast, then find the right people. My first MVP flopped, but it got me to my CTO, Anand. Sometimes failure is just a shortcut to the right partner.

Don't be afraid to build in public. People don't follow products. They follow stories. When your community feels ownership, they cheer for your success.

Listen > Assume. Our pivot from avatars to faceless video came from user feedback, not gut instinct. Ego kills companies. Data and listening save them.

ACTIONABLE TAKEAWAYS

Ask yourself the 20% question. If you're earning a small slice promoting someone else's product, could you build your own? List the gaps.

Run a "pain audit." Write down the top three most painful, repetitive tasks in your current business. Which one could be solved (or automated) with software?

Find your Anand. If tech isn't your strength, stop pretending it is. Identify one partner or hire who complements your weakness. I like to call this, "outsource your suck."

Document your build. Don't hide in stealth mode. Share updates, lessons, and failures publicly. Start small, even one LinkedIn post a week.

Plan your pivot muscle. Ask: if your current "hero feature" died tomorrow, what real problem would remain for your users? That's where your next evolution lies.

What were your 3 key takeaways:

_____

_____

_____

What 3 additional action steps are you going to take:

_____

_____

_____

What is the deadline you're setting for each of these steps:

_____

_____

_____

Chapter 9

Becoming An International Speaker

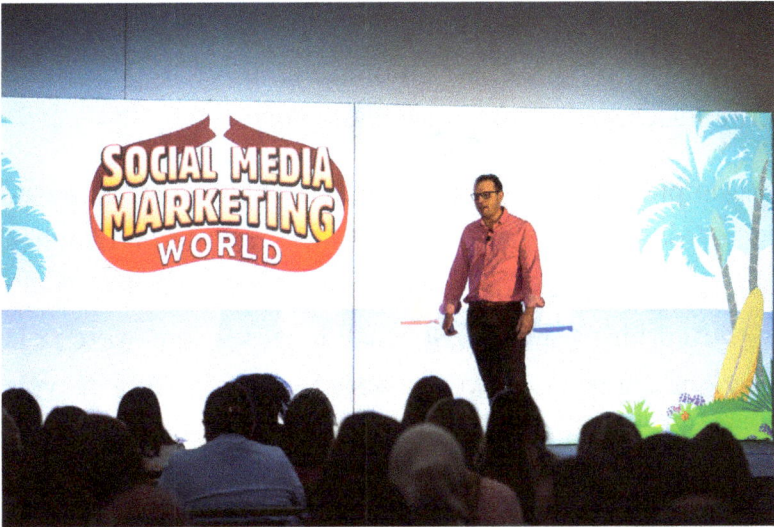

I knew early in my digital marketing journey that I wanted to be a speaker. Not just someone who popped up on the occasional panel, but the kind of speaker who could stand on any stage, anywhere in the world, and deliver value that moved people.

That dream felt huge at the time, maybe even unrealistic. But deep down, I knew I had something worth saying.

Ironically, my path to the stage didn't start on a stage. It started on video.

Before I ever held a mic, I had already recorded hundreds of videos. What I didn't realize then was that hitting "record" was quietly preparing me to be a speaker. Every video forced me to structure my thoughts, strip out the fluff, and deliver clearly. Video trained me to think like a communicator long before anyone called me one.

Back in 2017, I was working at a digital agency, and one of my jobs was generating new clients. I hated cold calling. I couldn't stand the idea of chasing people down who didn't want to hear from me. So instead, I tried something different: I hosted free lunch-and-learns for small business owners.

It was simple. I'd bring people together, share what I knew about digital marketing, answer their questions, and eat sandwiches. To my surprise, people showed up. And not only did they show up, they started hiring me. Those small local sessions weren't just a way to land clients; they were where I started finding my voice.

Soon after, I discovered Toastmasters. I'll never forget that first meeting. It wasn't glamorous, but it was practical. Toastmasters taught me to cut filler words, use silence intentionally, and tell stories that landed. It was the first time I felt like I was becoming a *speaker*, not just a guy who talked too much about marketing.

Then came TikTok.

When I launched my own agency in 2019, TikTok was blowing up. I leaned all the way in, and my audience grew fast. That's when the podcast invites started rolling in. Suddenly, I was being asked to share how I was growing on social media and turning content into a real business.

Every podcast became a mini stage. I sharpened my message, got better at thinking on my feet, and started building a reputation beyond my own channels.

And then came the message that changed everything.

In 2021, I cold-DM'd Scott Simson, founder of Video Marketing World, a conference I had attended as a guest and deeply admired. I didn't know him, but I figured, what's the worst that could happen?

Here's exactly what I wrote:

> Hey Scott! Pending it doesn't disappear lol, and you guys hopefully go back to doing in-person events for VMW. Would you be looking for TikTok for business speakers? I have ~46,000 followers on there specifically discussing digital marketing tips for small businesses, and it's been a massive profitable success for my own business. I have done some speaking in the past, and it's something I want to get more involved with. I would love to be a speaker at VMW if it makes sense when the world gets back to 'normal.'

To my surprise, Scott replied quickly. Not only did he say yes, he invited me on his livestream show. That was my foot in the door.

I gave the livestream everything I had. At the end, I shot my shot again:

> Scott, it's been a personal dream of mine to become a professional speaker. If you think I was good on the podcast, the opportunity to speak on stage would mean the world.

That led to my first real speaking gig: moderating a panel on TikTok for business. I prepared just like I would for a fight. I showed up early, stayed engaged all weekend, and networked like my life depended on it.

The next year, Scott invited me back, this time as a standalone keynote speaker.

And from there, doors opened. One stage led to another, and soon I was speaking internationally. Even now, with dozens of stages behind me and audiences of thousands, I still get nervous. Not because I'm scared, but because I care. Nervous energy means I'm about to do something that matters.

But the story didn't stop there. Scott and I became friends, collaborators, and eventually business partners. Today, we co-own *AI Marketing World,* the next evolution of the very conference that gave me my start. From a cold DM to keynote to co-owner, that's the power of shooting your shot.

If you've ever dreamed of becoming a speaker, here's what I'll tell you: you're enough, and your message is enough. Start where you are. Record that video. Host that free workshop. DM the organizer. Show up in the room. Show up without ego. Be prepared. Be consistent.

That's how you go from "who's this?" to "welcome to the stage."

GOLDEN NUGGETS

Video is a training ground for speaking. Recording hundreds of videos forces you to structure your thoughts, cut the fluff, and speak with clarity, skills that transfer directly to the stage.

Start small, think big. Local workshops and lunch-and-learns may feel minor, but they build confidence, sharpen delivery, and attract opportunities.

Every podcast is a mini stage. Treat interviews and small platforms like they're keynote stages. They train you for the bigger moments.

Shoot your shot. One cold DM to the right person can change everything. Opportunities often come when you're bold enough to ask.

Preparation signals respect. Overpreparing shows event organizers, audiences, and peers that you take the craft seriously, and it sets you apart.

Relationships create stages. Speaking isn't just about talent; it's about trust. Don't be an ego-filled diva; build relationships with organizers, peers, and communities.

ACTIONABLE TAKEAWAYS

Start on camera today. Record a short video sharing something you know. Post it, even if it's imperfect. Think of it as a rehearsal for the stage.

Host your own room. Organize a free workshop, webinar, or lunch-and-learn. Teaching live accelerates your speaking growth.

Say yes to podcasts. Even small shows matter. Treat every invite as practice for larger audiences.

Reach out to organizers. Identify one event or conference you admire and send a clear, respectful pitch. Don't wait for them to come to you.

Go to a local Toastmasters meeting. There are Toastmasters groups in almost every city. And the best part is you can go for free as a guest to see what it's all about. And if you're brave enough, volunteer to speak in front of the group on your first day.

Invest in relationships. Follow up with event hosts, thank them, share their work, and stay connected. This is how repeat invitations happen.

What were your 3 key takeaways:

_____

_____

_____

What 3 additional action steps are you going to take:

_____

_____

_____

What is the deadline you're setting for each of these steps:

_____

_____

_____

Chapter 10

Over 1 million Views With Faceless YouTube Channel

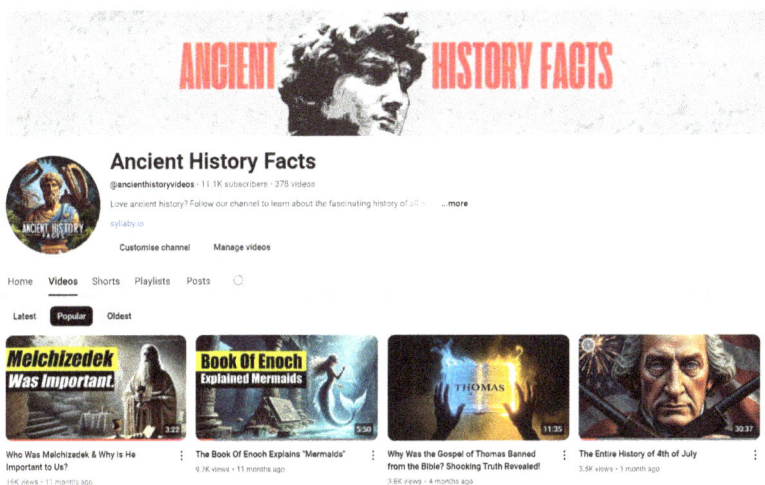

The dream of growing a YouTube or social media channel without ever showing your face? That's something SO many people fantasize about. And that's exactly where the concept of faceless videos comes in.

But here's the challenge I want to give you up front: get out of your own way and just be the face of your content. Harsh? Maybe. But hear me out. The truth is, no one cares what you look like.

They're not paying attention to the blemish on your cheek or the way your hair flops weirdly in the front. And even if someone does leave a snarky comment, if your mental health can handle it, guess what? They just helped your engagement algorithm. (We'll talk more about engagement hacking and how to actually increase your haters, yes, on purpose, in a later chapter.)

People care about value. That's it. We are always our own worst critics, and if fear of being on camera is what's stopping you from showing up... well, this book is your permission slip to stop caring and start creating.

That said, if you absolutely can't, or won't, get on camera, I've got good news. You can still reap the rewards of content creation without ever pressing record on your front-facing camera.

Faceless videos have exploded across the internet. I see them racking up millions (sometimes tens of millions) of views every single day. Topics like ancient history, conspiracy theories, personal finance, and crime stories perform especially well in this format.

So, what exactly are faceless videos? As the name suggests, they're videos that don't show anyone's face on camera. Think: narrator voice-over, relevant B-roll, animations, or slides. Basically, documentary-style storytelling. Until recently, making these kinds of videos required a lot of manual effort: writing scripts, gathering B-roll, editing, adding voiceover, subtitles, and music.

And then came AI.

Thanks to automation, the entire process of making faceless videos can now be streamlined end-to-end. At my company, , we produce over 2,000 faceless videos every single day.

And this all started... on a road trip.

I was driving from Durham, North Carolina, to Alexandria, Virginia, my wife asleep in the passenger seat, when I called my co-founder and CTO, Anand. We ended up on the phone for over two hours, brainstorming how to automate the entire video creation pipeline: from idea to publishing.

Mile after mile, we mapped it out: what tech we'd need, where the current tools fell short, what creators actually wanted. We laughed at the clunky competitors in the space and started sketching out a solution that felt bold, but doable.

That conversation? It saved our company.

The reality was: we were on the ropes.

When we first launched Syllaby, we shot to $88k/month in recurring revenue in under 7 months. I thought we had cracked the code. But then the market shifted. The avatar tech wasn't ready. Competitors popped up everywhere. Users weren't staying. They were "AI tourists," hopping from one tool to the next.

I'll never forget opening our Stripe dashboard and watching the numbers sink: $88k... $70k... $50k... until we were barely hanging on above $35k (see picture in Chapter 8). It was like getting punched in the gut, over and over again.

We had employees counting on us. Families counting on us. My stomach dropped every time I refreshed those numbers. It felt like everything we had built was crumbling, and that maybe, we were done.

But we weren't done. Not yet.

We went on to build what I believe is the best faceless video tool on the internet. Syllaby shows you trending topics in any niche, writes scripts (long or short form), generates AI-animated videos in over 40 art styles, adds voiceovers, subtitles, background music, and even publishes across all major platforms.

Let me say that again: you can now automate an entire month of video content in minutes.

And of course, I use it myself.

One of my faceless YouTube channels, *Ancient History Facts*, racked up over a million views and 11,000+ subscribers in just a few months. (Probably more by the time you're reading this.) Here's the exact strategy I used to get there:

- I researched the top-performing videos in my niche.

- I studied the best-performing titles.

- I recreated those videos using Syllaby, keeping a similar structure and title formula.

- If a video outperformed the average (e.g., 10k views vs. 1k), I turned it into a series.

In fact, one of my most successful series is titled *"Real Facts Confirmed in the Bible."* I've used that title on over 40 Shorts. And guess what? Most of them outperformed my other videos. (Yes, it's okay to reuse a title that works. Just don't do it for long-form content.)

	Short		Visibility	Restrictions	Date	Views ↓
☐		Real Confirmed Facts In The Bible This video was made entirely using https://www.syllaby.io	🌐 Public	None	14 Jul 2024 Published	13,234
☐		Real Confirmed Facts In The Bible This video was created entirely with https://www.syllaby.io Try it yourself!	🌐 Public	None	15 Jul 2024 Published	12,208
☐		Real Confirmed Facts In The Bible This video was created entirely with https://www.syllaby.io Try it yourself!	🌐 Public	None Shorts policy	18 Jul 2024 Published	12,111
☐		Real Confirmed Facts In The Bible This video was made entirely using https://www.syllaby.io	🌐 Public	None	1 Aug 2024 Published	11,976
☐		Real Confirmed Facts In The Bible This video was made entirely using https://www.syllaby.io	🌐 Public	None	13 Jul 2024 Published	11,078
☐		Real Facts Confirmed in The Bible This video was made using https://www.syllaby.io Make faceless videos like this on any topic in less than 3 minutes!	🌐 Public	None	22 Jan 2025 Published	10,010
☐		Real facts confirmed in the dead sea scrolls This video was made using https://www.syllaby.io Make faceless videos like this on any topic in less than 3 minutes!	🌐 Public	None	14 Aug 2024 Published	9,847
☐		Real Confirmed Facts In The Bible This video was created entirely with https://www.syllaby.io Try	🌐 Public	None	23 Jul 2024 Published	9,243

And here's the kicker: at the end of every single video, I include a strong call-to-action:

"Subscribe if you love The Bible."

"Subscribe if you love [insert niche here]."

I know that title strategy goes against what most YouTube coaches preach. But I've tested it hundreds of times. It works. For me. For my clients. Across industries.

This approach, combined with the power of AI and automation, has helped drive hundreds of millions of organic views.

So if you're serious about building a faceless channel, I've got one final piece of advice: Start now. Don't wait for perfection. Don't wait for someone to give you permission. The tools are here. The audience is watching. And if I can build something like this from a car ride conversation, so can you.

Go create.

GOLDEN NUGGETS

Your face isn't the barrier. Fear is. The market doesn't care about your insecurities. People show up for *value*, not your jaw-line or your lighting. Even hate fuels the algorithm.

Faceless content is more than a trend. It's an entry point. For creators unwilling or unable to be on camera, faceless video is a proven, scalable lane. Entire industries thrive here.

A video series can build compounding momentum. One hit video is luck. Turning it into a repeatable *series* creates audience habits and a reason to come back, which turns random views into long-term growth.

Identity-driven CTAs beat generic pitches. "Subscribe if you love The Bible" outperforms "Like and Subscribe" because it connects to belonging, not obligation.

ACTIONABLE TAKEAWAYS

Face the camera once. Even if you *think* you'll go faceless, record one short talking-head video. The process will either free you from fear or confirm that faceless is your true lane.

Pick your battlefield. Choose a niche where faceless thrives: history, conspiracy, finance, crime, spirituality. Don't dabble, commit.

Audit the winners. Study your niche's top videos. Steal the structure. Mirror the title formulas. Don't reinvent, reverse-engineer.

Double down on spikes. If a video gets 10x your average views, immediately turn it into a series. Don't let momentum die, ride the wave.

Automate to survive. Use tools like to script, edit, and publish at scale. If you try to do everything manually, you might burn out before you break through.

Close with identity. Replace "Like and Subscribe" with a niche identity CTA. Speak to who your viewer *is* or who they want to be.

What were your 3 key takeaways:

_____

_____

_____

What 3 additional action steps are you going to take:

_____

_____

_____

What is the deadline you're setting for each of these steps:

_____

_____

_____

PART 2: Tactical Strategies. It's Go Time.

Welcome to the back half of the book.

If Part 1 gave you clarity, sparked new ideas, and lit a fire under you, perfect. That was the point. But clarity without action is wasted potential. Now it's time to build.

This is where inspiration meets execution. Chapter by chapter, I'll break down the exact tools, systems, and workflows I'm using right now to grow brands, automate content, and scale income streams. No fluff. No theory. Just tested strategies that have helped me (and my clients) reach millions of followers, rack up billions of views, and generate millions in revenue from organic social media.

Now, fair warning: some of these strategies might stretch you. They may challenge how you think about content. They might even make you uncomfortable. Good. That's where growth happens. If you do what everyone else is doing, you'll end up with the same results everyone else is getting.

Quick caveat: nothing here is a magic bullet. Algorithms change. Platforms evolve. What works today might look different tomorrow. But the underlying principles, consistency, creativity, and commitment, don't change. If you stay in motion and play the long game, these strategies will stack the odds massively in your favor.

And one more thing: Don't just read these chapters. Use them. And write down **your** next steps and timeline. Implement fast. Start messy if you have to, but start.

This is your playbook. This is where the real work begins. Let's get tactical. Let's get to work. Let's go.

Chapter 11

The S.T.A.R.T. Video Framework

S.T.A.R.T.

Video Framework

- Stop the scroll with a powerful opening hook
- Talk about a problem your target audience is dealing with
- Align with your audience to build credibility and trust
- Resolve the problem with actionable "FREE" advice
- Tell them what to do next! (Your CTA)

Over the last 12 years in video marketing and production, I've created and published more than 10,000 videos across social media. Translation: I've failed a lot. Some videos I spent weeks (and thousands of dollars) producing completely flopped. Others, filmed on my phone in 30 minutes, went viral.

Those failures and wins taught me something: virality is not luck. It's repeatable. That's why I built the **S.T.A.R.T. Video Frame-**

work, a system I've tested in nearly every industry. And when used consistently, it stacks the odds heavily in your favor.

Will every video go viral? No. But this framework will make your content impossible to ignore, especially if you're a business owner who wants leads and sales, not just likes.

Here's how it works:

S. Stop the Scroll with a Powerful Hook

This is the single most important part of a successful video. We live in an era of **ultra-short attention spans** fueled by endless scrolling. With one swipe of a thumb, a new video appears. If you don't grab attention in the first **2–3 seconds**, you lose.

And yet, here's how most people start their videos:

"Hi everyone, my name is [name]. I'm a [job title] with X years of experience, and today I'm going to talk about..."

STOP IT.

No one cares. Seriously. Social media isn't where people come to learn about *you*. They come for **entertainment, distraction, or education.** Your job is to earn their attention before you can earn their trust.

So how do you do it? Think of your hook like the **front-page headline of a magazine**. Its only purpose is to interrupt their pattern and make them curious enough to keep watching.

Hooks can be **audible** (what you say) or **visual** (what they see). For example:

- *Visual hook*: Start hammering a nail into a tire while saying, "Everyone asks me how to change a tire." (Viewers instantly think: WTF is happening?)

- *Audible hook*: Use a bold, exaggerated opener like...

  - "These 5 websites feel illegal to know."

  - "Marketers don't want you to know this ChatGPT hack."

  - "This AI tool will scare you."

  - "Canva is about to DESTROY Photoshop."

Yes, they're dramatic. That's the point. They make people stop scrolling. I've used hooks like these hundreds of times, and together, they've pulled in **billions of views**.

But it doesn't stop with AI/software. These frameworks can work for *any business* when adapted to your niche:

- "I can't believe nobody is talking about this..."

- "Here's how I [achieved result] in [timeframe] without [common obstacle]."

- "Stop doing this one thing, it's hurting your [results/goals]."

- "Most people have no idea this exists..."

- "I found the [topic] cheat code."

- "This is how [well-known company/person] is achieving [X result], you can copy it."

- "If I had to start from scratch today, here's exactly what I'd do."

- "This one tiny change made a massive difference..."

- "I wish I knew this when I started."

- "You've been lied to about [topic], here's the truth."

Key principle: Your hook must make the viewer feel one of three things:

1. *Curiosity* – "Wait, what?"

2. *Urgency* – "I need to know this now."

3. *Shock/surprise* – "That can't be true."

If your opening doesn't spark one of those emotions, they'll swipe away and never come back.

T. Talk About a Problem or Emotional Pain Point

You've grabbed their attention with a hook. Now what? Now you **qualify** them to keep watching. This is where most creators drop the ball.

Here's the truth: people are scrolling for a reason. They're looking for...

- **Solutions** to their problems

- **Distractions** from their problems

- **Education** to help them level up

Your job here is to tap into the thing that's keeping them up at night. What frustrates them daily? What are they secretly afraid of? What feels impossible right now?

Most creators make the mistake of staying vague:

"Buying a house is hard." "Back pain sucks."

That's not enough. You need to dig **deep into the pain**. Make them feel seen. Make them think: *"This person is literally inside my head."*

Example 1: Real Estate

- Hook: *"The housing market is about to crash."*

- Pain: *"You've been saving for years, watching prices climb higher every month. Every time you think you finally have enough for a down payment, the goalpost moves. You're stuck paying someone else's mortgage through rent while your friends are building equity. You're terrified. If you buy now, you could lose everything. But if you wait, you might never get in at all."*

Example 2: Fitness

- Hook: *"The one exercise that's destroying your back."*

- Pain: *"Every morning you wake up feeling like you're 80. That sharp pain shoots down your leg when you bend to tie your shoes. You've tried chiropractors, massage, stretching, spent thousands, but nothing sticks. You can't even play with your kids without wincing. And the scariest thought? This might just be your life now."*

See the difference? Specific pain points hit harder than general statements.

Common Emotional Triggers to Pull On:

- Fear of missing out (*everyone else is succeeding but me*)

- Fear of failure (*what if I waste my time and money?*)

- Frustration with complexity (*why is this so complicated?*)

- Overwhelm (*too much info, don't know where to start*)

- Skepticism (*I've tried everything, nothing works*)

- Imposter syndrome (*who am I to do this?*)

- Time pressure (*I'm running out of time to fix this*)

Example 3: AI Tools

- Hook: *"ChatGPT is about to replace your job."*

- Pain: *"Every day, another AI tool pops up. Your coworkers*

are using them. Your competitors are using them. Mean-
while, you're still doing everything manually... 10x slower.
You know you need to learn this stuff, but every tutorial
assumes you're already tech-savvy. You try, you get over-
whelmed, you quit. Deep down, you're scared that if you
don't figure it out soon, you'll be irrelevant."

That's the level of specificity you need.

Rule of thumb:

- Generic problems = generic engagement.

- Specific problems = "This person gets me."

Pain-Point Script Builder

Use this formula to describe your audience's struggle in a way that makes them feel like you're reading their mind:

"You feel [negative emotion] every time you [frustrating situation]. You've tried [failed attempts], but [why it didn't work]. Now you're worried that [scary consequence]."

Examples by Industry:

Real Estate: "You feel defeated every time you check housing prices. You've tried saving for years, but every time you're close, the market jumps again. Now you're worried you'll never afford a home."

Fitness: "You feel frustrated every time you look in the mirror. You've tried fad diets and expensive programs, but the weight always comes back. Now you're worried nothing will ever work for you."

Business/Entrepreneurship: "You feel overwhelmed every time you open your laptop. You've tried dozens of marketing strategies, but none have brought consistent sales. Now you're worried you'll never break out of this cycle."

AI/Tech: "You feel left behind every time someone mentions a new AI tool. You've tried watching tutorials, but they're confusing and assume you're an expert. Now you're worried AI is going to replace you before you catch up."

Pro tip: The more **specific** your details, the more your audience feels, *"That's exactly me."* That emotional connection is what makes them keep watching.

A. Align with Your Audience (Build Credibility & Trust)

This step is about proving you're worth listening to, without boring them. You have **5-10 seconds max** to show credibility. Not your life story. Not your resume. A quick credibility drop that makes them lean in.

The mistake most people make? Spending 30 seconds rambling:

"Hi, I'm [name]. I've been doing this for 18 years, I started on MySpace, I've worked with hundreds of clients, I have 2.7M followers, I speak at conferences..."

STOP IT. Nobody cares.

Instead, **make it about them, not you.** Tie your credibility directly to the problem they're facing:

- "I've helped 347 real estate agents close over $2M in commissions using this exact strategy."

- "After analyzing over 10,000 viral videos, I discovered the pattern."

- "My clients used to struggle with this same issue until we implemented this system."

- "I spent $50,000 testing Facebook ads so you don't have to."

- "Last month alone, 23 businesses doubled their leads with this method."

Notice how every credential is positioned as a benefit for THEM.

Credibility Builders That Work:

- **Specific numbers** - Not "I've helped lots of people," but "I've helped 1,247 entrepreneurs."

- **Relevant results** - If you're teaching weight loss, "I helped John go from 246 lbs to 165 lbs in 6 months."

- **Transformation stories** - "One student went from 0 to 100K followers in 90 days using this."

- **Costly mistakes** - "This mistake cost me 3 years and 900,000 followers on TikTok, don't repeat it." (This actually happened to me personally).

- **Pattern recognition** - "After analyzing every viral video in my niche for 3 years, here's what I found."

Good vs. Bad Alignment Statements:

- **Bad:** "I'm a certified personal trainer with 10 years of experience." **Good:** "I've helped 500+ people lose over 20,000 pounds combined using this method."

- **Bad:** "I'm a successful entrepreneur with multiple six-figure businesses." **Good:** "This strategy generated $2.3M for my agency last year."

- **Bad:** "I'm an expert in social media marketing." **Good:** "My videos have been viewed over 500 million times using this exact framework."

But what if you don't have big credentials yet? That's fine. Use what you *do* have:

- "I tested this on my own account and gained 5,000 followers in a week."

- "I'm documenting my journey step by step."

- "I spent 100 hours researching this so you don't have to."

- "I interviewed 50 experts to get the answer."

The point isn't perfection, it's proof. Show them you're not guessing. You've done the work.

Credibility Drop Formula

"I've [done specific action/result] so that [audience] can [benefit]."

This keeps your authority short, sharp, and audience-focused.

Examples by Industry:

Marketing/Business

- "I've analyzed 10,000 viral videos so that entrepreneurs can finally crack the algorithm."

- "I've helped 347 real estate agents close over $2M in commissions so they could stop stressing about where their next client would come from."

Fitness

- "I've helped 500+ people lose over 20,000 pounds combined so they could feel confident in their own skin again."

- "I tested this routine myself and built 20 pounds of muscle so that busy dads can train smarter, not longer."

Tech/AI

- "I spent $50,000 testing Facebook ads so that small business owners don't have to burn cash figuring it out."

- "I documented my journey learning AI tools so that beginners can shortcut months of trial and error."

Coaching/Personal Development

- "I've coached 1,200 people through career changes so they can finally do work they love."

- "I interviewed 50 experts on burnout so busy professionals can reclaim their energy without quitting their jobs."

Quick Plug-and-Play Template

Fill in the blanks:

- "I've [tested/tried/studied/analyzed] _ _ _ so that _ _ _ can _ _ _."

- "I've [helped/supported/worked with] _ _ _ so they could _ _ _."

- "I've [failed/lost/spent] _ _ _ so you don't have to _ _ _."

Pro Tip: If you don't have huge numbers yet, lean on:

- Effort invested —> "I spent 100 hours researching this..."

- Personal experiment —> "I tested this on myself and got _ _ _ result."

- Community borrowed proof —> "I interviewed _ _ _ people so you can _ _ _."

R. Resolve the Problem with Actionable "Free" Advice

One of the best lessons I've ever learned in marketing:**Give your best information away for free. Sell the implementation.**

This is where you deliver the goods, the solution to the exact problem you just exposed.

But let's be clear: I don't mean vague advice like "work harder," "stay consistent," or "believe in yourself." That's motivational fluff. Your audience doesn't need fluff. They need **steps they can apply right now.**

Here's the rule: **If someone can't take your advice and get a result within 24 hours, your advice sucks.**

Bad vs. Good Advice Examples

- **Bad:** "To grow on social media, you need to post consistently." **Good:** "Here's exactly how to grow on social media:

    a. Go to AnswerThePublic.com and type in your industry.

    b. Pick 5 questions people are asking.

    c. Create one video per question using this format: Hook —> Problem —> Solution —> Call to Action.

    d. Post at 8am, 12pm, or 5pm (my testing shows +23% engagement).

    e. Use hashtags #useful #business #websites #marketingtips.

f. Respond to every comment in the first hour; algorithms love it."

- **Bad:** "Improve your website SEO." **Good:** "Install the Yoast SEO plugin. Check every page until the light turns green. Then open Google Search Console, find your top 10 pages, and add 500 words of content targeting queries you're already close to ranking for."

- **Bad:** "Use AI to save time." **Good:** "Go to ChatGPT, use this exact prompt: *'You are an expert copywriter. Write me 10 hooks for a video about [topic] using the S.T.A.R.T. framework.'* Take the best one, ask for a 60-second script, then copy it into Syllaby.io to generate a full video in 5 minutes."

- **Bad:** "Network more to grow your business." **Good:** "Join 3 Facebook groups in your niche. Every Mon/Wed/Fri, answer 5 questions in each group with helpful advice (never pitch). Add a signature that says: *'DM me if you need more help.'* I average 20–30 leads a week from this."

Why this works: When you give away specific, actionable advice, people test it. They get results. That builds **know, like, and trust.**

- They **know** you because you keep showing up in their feed.

- They **like** you because you're generous and relatable.

- They **trust** you because your free stuff actually worked.

And when they're ready to buy? You're the obvious choice.

Think of it like cooking: Gordon Ramsay could give you his exact beef wellington recipe, step by step. Will yours taste like his? No. But you'll make something better than you had before, you'll trust the recipe, and when you want the *real* thing, you'll book a table at his restaurant.

How to Structure Your Solution

When you deliver advice, use this simple structure:

1. **The What** - *Here's what to do.*

2. **The How** - *Here's how to do it step by step.*

3. **The Why** - *Here's why it works.*

4. **The Example** - *Here's what it looks like in practice.*

5. **The Shortcut** - *Here's a tool/template/resource to make it easier.*

Example (Email Marketing):

- **What:** Send 3 emails per week.

- **How:** Monday = Educational, Wednesday = Case Study, Friday = Promotion.

- **Why:** This cadence keeps you top of mind without being annoying.

- **Example:** "Monday: '5 ways to improve your subject lines.'

Wednesday: Share how a client got 10K opens. Friday: Promote your course."

- **Shortcut:** "Grab my 30 plug-and-play email templates at the link in my bio."

Pro Tip: If you're worried about giving away too much, you're not giving away enough.

I've literally given away:

- The funnel that makes me six figures in affiliate commissions

- The script formula that built 4M followers

- The engagement hacks I still use today

- The prompts and strategies I used to launch micro-SaaS tools

And guess what? People still pay me to implement, because there's a massive difference between **information** and **implementation.**

T. Tell them what to do next! (Your call to action)

You want leads, sales, and ROI from your social media efforts, I assume, yes?

Here's the brutal truth: great content without a call to action is just entertainment. You hooked them. You identified their pain. You built trust. You delivered actionable advice. Now what?

If you don't tell people what to do next, they'll scroll away and forget about you by tomorrow. That's not what we're building here. You're building a business, not a hobby.

Your call to action is the bridge between content and cash flow. It turns views into value, attention into action, and followers into customers. Without it, you're leaving money on the table.

The Golden Rule: ONE clear call to action.

Not three. Not five. ONE.

People have analysis paralysis. If you tell them "smash that like button, follow for more, click the link in my bio and tag 3 friends!" Guess what? They're not going to do anything.

Instead, give them one intentional call to action per video. Here are some examples.

Bad vs. Good Calls to Action

Bad: "Check out my website, follow me on Instagram, subscribe to my YouTube, and join my Facebook group for more tips!"
Good: "Comment TOOL and I'll DM you the link."

Bad: "If you want to learn more about this, you can find some resources in my bio, or you can Google it, or just let me know in the comments."

Good: "Link in my bio for the complete tutorial and free template."

Bad: "Thanks for watching! See you next time!"
Good: "If you found this helpful, join my free weekly newsletter at the link in my bio. I share tools and tutorials like this every week."

Bad: "Let me know what you think in the comments below and don't forget to like and subscribe if you enjoyed this video."
Good: "Follow for daily AI tools that'll save you 10 hours a week."

Bad: "You can find my course on my website if you're interested in learning more about this topic."
Good: "Click the link in my bio to grab my free checklist of 20 AI prompts that'll change how you work."

See the difference? Good CTAs are specific, direct, and action-oriented. They tell people exactly what to do and what they'll get.

The Most Effective Calls to Action

Here are the CTAs that generate the most leads and sales for me:

1. Comment trigger word for automation

"Comment BOOM and I'll DM you the link."

Use tools like ManyChat or Go High Level to automatically respond. This drives massive engagement, works while you sleep, and every comment becomes a lead in your CRM. I've generated thousands of direct messages using this one tactic.

2. Link in bio

"Link in my bio for the full tutorial."

Use a bio tool like LinkTree, Beacons, or Stan Store to organize multiple links. Update it weekly. Keep it clean and simple. This is your digital storefront. Make it easy to navigate.

3. Newsletter opt-in

"If you found this helpful, join my free weekly newsletter for more tips and tools."

This is how I grow my list by 100-200 subscribers daily. Your email list is your most valuable asset. Social platforms can disappear tomorrow. Your email list is yours forever.

4. Direct to landing page

"Click the link to grab my free resource."

Give away a lead magnet: a checklist, template, or list of tools. Exchange value for their email. Then nurture that relationship through email sequences.

5. Follow or subscribe

"Follow for daily content like this."

Sounds basic, but people need to be reminded. Don't assume they'll do it automatically. Ask clearly and directly.

How to Make Your CTA Impossible to Miss

Most people bury their CTA at the end of a caption or mumble it quickly. WRONG.

Your CTA needs to be visible, repeated, and unavoidable:

Say it out loud in the video

Put it in on-screen text or subtitles

Make it the first line in your caption so it appears above the fold

Pin it as the top comment if the platform allows

Repeat it at the end of the video

The more visible your CTA, the more conversions you get. Period.

The Psychology Behind CTAs

People need direction. They're busy, distracted, scrolling fast. If you don't tell them what to do, they won't do anything.

Guide them clearly, confidently, and with urgency:

Use action verbs: Comment. Click. Download. Join. Subscribe.

Create urgency: "This offer ends Friday." "Only 50 spots available."

Remove friction: "Takes 10 seconds." "Completely free." "No credit card required."

Show the benefit: "Save 5 hours a week." "Instant access." "Results in 24 hours."

Stop Being Timid

Here's the misconception: people think asking for something is pushy.

It's not.

You just gave them 60 seconds of incredible free value. You solved a problem. You taught them something useful. Asking them to follow you, join your list, or try a tool is not pushy. It's helpful.

You're doing them a favor by making it easy to stay connected and get more value.

CTA Script Builder

Use this formula for every video:

"[Action verb] + [What they'll get] + [Where to do it]"

Examples by Industry:

Marketing/Business:
"Comment STRATEGY and I'll send you my free 5-step marketing checklist."

Fitness:
"Click the link in my bio to download my 7-day meal plan, completely free."

Real Estate:
"Follow for daily market updates that'll help you buy your first home."

AI/Tech:
"Link in bio for my free list of 50 AI tools that'll transform how you work."

Coaching:
"Comment GROWTH and I'll DM you my free guide to landing your first 5 clients."

Every piece of content should move someone closer to becoming a lead, subscriber, or customer. Without a clear CTA, you're just creating content for vanity metrics.

Your call to action is not optional. It's the entire point.

So go back through the S.T.A.R.T. framework. Apply it to your next video. Make your CTA clear, direct, and impossible to ignore.

Because here's the reality: consistency beats perfection. Action beats planning. Momentum beats hesitation.

You don't need to be perfect. You just need to START.

What were your 3 key takeaways:

_____

_____

_____

What 3 additional action steps are you going to take:

_____

_____

_____

What is the deadline you're setting for each of these steps:

_____

_____

_____

Chapter 12

Engagement Hacks That Actually Work

Let me hit you with something blunt: you're probably doing social media wrong.

You're playing it safe. You're posting nice, polite content. You're trying not to ruffle feathers. And then you wonder why your engagement is flatlined.

This chapter is going to push you out of your comfort zone. Some of what I'm about to share will feel controversial, maybe even manipulative. That's intentional. Because here's the brutal truth: if you want real engagement, you can't just hope people will comment, you need to engineer it.

Positive comments, negative comments, it doesn't matter. Engagement is engagement, and the algorithm doesn't care why people are interacting. It only cares that they are.

So if you're ready to stop being invisible and start being impossible to ignore, keep reading.

The Psychology Behind Why This Works

After years of testing and billions of views, I've discovered some-thing most creators won't admit: it's *easier to get negative engage-ment than positive engagement.*

Think about it. Social media platforms are designed around this truth, but you see it every day offline, too.

How many times have you been to a restaurant that was just... fine? The food was okay, the service was decent, nothing spectacular, nothing awful. Did you sprint to Google to leave them a glowing 5-star review for being average? Of course not.

But when the service is rude, the food comes out cold, or you find a hair in your meal, you can't wait to tell someone about it. You'll warn your friends, leave a scathing review, maybe even post about it. Negative experiences trigger us faster and louder than neutral ones.

The opposite is also true. When something is *exceptional*, flawless food, amazing service, an unforgettable experience, we love to praise and share it. But that level of excellence is rare.

On social media, the same principle applies:

- When people agree with you, they usually just hit "like" and keep scrolling.

- When they *disagree*, when you poke their worldview, mis-pronounce a word, state something bold, or make a "mis-take", they *stop everything* to tell you why you're wrong.

Their ego demands it.

And the algorithm doesn't care whether comments are "You're brilliant" or "You're an idiot." It just sees engagement. More comments. More time spent on the post. More signals that your content is worth boosting.

So here's my challenge to you: instead of fighting this, why not lean into it? Engineer the triggers that make people stop, comment, argue, and share. That's how you hack engagement at scale.

Strategy 1: Planting a "WTF?!" Easter Egg

Take a deep breath. This strategy is where some people tap out. But if you get it, you'll understand why it works. And don't worry, I'll give you a more PG version in a second.

If you've watched my videos where I show websites, you may have noticed something odd. Ever catch a weird folder name below the URL bar? Or a strange tab open at the top? I plant these little "Easter eggs" on purpose, folders labeled things like *"Mr. Beast Nud..."* or *"Where to hide a dead body."* I never mention them. They just sit there, in plain sight, daring viewers to notice.

And without fail, they do. Every single time. Comments flood in:

- *"WTF is that folder?!"*

- *"That tab looks suspicious..."*

- Or even texts from friends telling me, *"Austin, you might want to delete that video."*

Got 'em.

Here's the magic: while people are rushing to the comments to point out the "mistake," the video keeps playing in the background, boosting my watch time. Their comments spark replies. Replies spark threads. Suddenly, the algorithm thinks my video is hot, and it gets pushed to even more people.

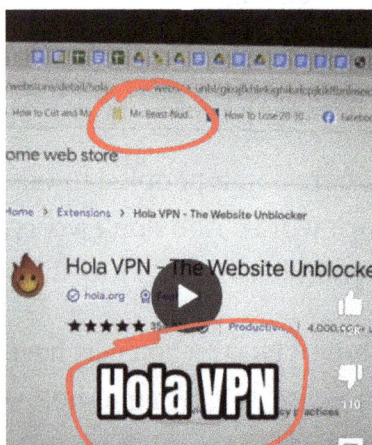

Trolls are inevitable online. My strategy? Troll the trolls. I plant engagement traps that fuel the algorithm while I keep delivering valuable, helpful content. Now, you don't need to go as extreme as me. Easter eggs don't have to be risqué. They just have to spark curiosity.

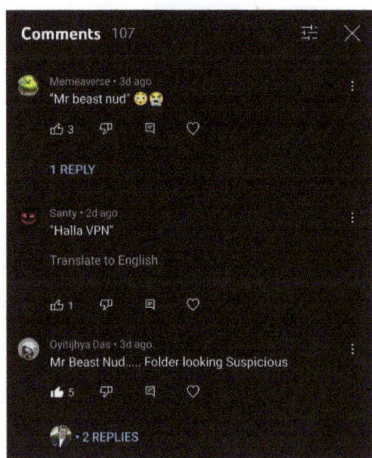

The real goal is to build a tribe that "gets the joke." These are the people who start defending you in the comments, saying things like

"First time here, huh?"

when new viewers freak out. That's when you know you've built something special.

PG Easter Egg Ideas:

- Place a quirky item in the background of your videos, something that shows your personality.

- Have a team member in a Bigfoot costume walk through the background during real estate videos without a word. *Bigfoot House Tours*

- A client of mine hid a stuffed animal called Wolfie in every video. Viewers made a game out of spotting him. *Where's Wolfie*

Strategy 2: The Intentional Mispronunciation

This one's sneaky, and it works every single time.

As an example, I'll create a video about a website called **AnswerSocrates.com**, which shows you the exact questions people are searching for online. But instead of pronouncing it correctly, I'll deliberately say: *"Answer So-Krat-us dot com."*

Within minutes, the comments exploded:

- *"How dare you butcher Socrates' name!"*

- *"It's SOCK-rah-teez, not So-krat-us!"*

- *"Did this guy even go to school?"*

And here's the kicker: some people even defend my pronunciation, sparking full-blown **comment wars**. Suddenly, a video that might have gotten 20 likes and 3 comments is racking up hundreds of comments and thousands of extra views.

It's the **GIF vs. JIF debate** all over again, a manufactured controversy that fuels the algorithm. And the best part? While they're arguing in the comments, they're also still watching my content and absorbing the actual value.

The lesson? Don't be afraid to engineer small, harmless "mistakes" that people can't resist correcting. Their ego does the engagement work for you.

Strategy 3: Make Bold, Black and White Statements

Nuance doesn't drive engagement; certainty does.

We live in a complex world, but when it comes to social media, the more black-and-white your statement, the more people feel compelled to react.

I'll post something like *"I'm team Android,"* and instantly the Apple fanboys rush in, ready to go to war. Or I'll say, *"Don't be afraid to work for free to get your foot in the door."* Half the comments scream "worker exploitation!" while the other half share how working for free landed them life-changing opportunities.

And that's the point. When you make a bold, definitive statement, you **force people to pick a side**. They can't just scroll past. They feel the need to argue, defend, or double down in agreement.

Here's another quick example you can try: Just say anything positive or negative about Elon Musk or Donald Trump. It doesn't matter what side you're on. Just make an absolute claim. Your engagement will explode. (Thick skin is necessary.)

Here's the key: **pick a side and stick to it.** If you try to appeal to everyone, you'll connect with no one. The stronger your stance, the stronger the reaction. And strong reactions = strong engagement.

Strategy 4: Bait Your Trolls To Keep Commenting

Let's be real, **trolls are inevitable.** If you've been creating content for more than five minutes, you already know this. The difference is how you handle them. Most creators get upset, clap back in anger, or ignore them completely and just block them. I do something different: I *bait them to keep talking.*

When a troll leaves a snarky comment, I don't fight back. I ask them questions. I'll say, *"Interesting point, can you explain what you mean?"* or *"So what would you do differently?"* Before they know it, they've left five more comments arguing their case. That's five more signals to the algorithm that my content is worth promoting.

Sometimes I'll even end the exchange with a wink: *"Congrats, you just helped me boost this video's reach. I just taught you a free engagement lesson."*

Here's the beauty of it:

1. Their negativity fuels *more visibility* for my content.

2. Since my page is monetized, I literally **get paid from their hate.**

The key is to keep your tone playful, not petty. Stay unbothered. Let them burn their energy while you reap the rewards.

The Mindset Shift You Need to Make

Stop thinking like a **content creator.** Start thinking like an **entrepreneur who creates content.** There's a massive difference.

Content creators worry about likes, views, and whether their hair looked good on camera. Entrepreneurs focus on impact, revenue, and using content as a vehicle to grow their business.

And here's the reality about negative comments: **they're never really about you.** They're about the troll's own insecurity. Most of them don't even have a profile picture. They're "username_47365" with zero content, hiding behind the keyboard while you're putting yourself out there.

You're doing the courageous thing; they're not. They're jealous you had the guts to press "publish" when they never will.

So if you're self-conscious about how you look, how you sound, or whether you know "enough", get over it. Your perspective matters. Your voice matters. And the marketplace rewards those willing to show up, not those who hide.

Your content does not need to be perfect. Leveraging these tactics will get you more reach, inspire more people, and ultimately more sales.

Algorithm Manipulation Principles

Let's cut the fluff: every platform is powered by **engagement signals.** The sooner you learn to engineer those signals on purpose, the sooner you'll blow past your competition.

Here's the playbook:

- **Curiosity Hooks:** Use phrases like *"What no one tells you..."* or *"You've probably never thought of this..."* to spark that "I have to know" instinct.

- **Watch Time Magnets:** Keep people glued with quick cuts, humor, pattern interrupts, and hooks layered throughout the video. Attention = currency.

- **Momentum Through Series:** Don't just post one-off content. Create Part 1, Part 2, Part 3. Series force binge-watching, which the algorithm loves.

  - Personal Example: I recently started a ChatGPT "Secrets You Should Know series" that I currently have 19 parts for.

- **Social Proof Flex:** Drop lines like *"This strategy got me 100K followers in 30 days"* to validate your authority and make people lean in.

- **Emotional Connection:** Solve real, painful problems. "Struggling to get clients?" hits harder than "Here are some marketing tips."

The algorithm isn't magic. It's math. Feed it the signals it craves consistently, and it will reward you with reach, followers, and revenue.

The Ethics Question

I know what you're thinking: *"Isn't this manipulation?"*

You're going to get trolls no matter what. Social media is built for conflict. It practically manufactures it. I'm not inventing negativity, I'm simply being **strategic about directing it** while still delivering massive value. Don't hate the player. Hate the game. I'm just trying to play the game at its highest level.

The key is balance. Find what you feel comfortable with that you can include in most or all of your videos to trigger some emotional response. It can be positive. It can be negative. As long as the content that you create genuinely helps someone. When your audience consistently learns, grows, and wins because of your content, they'll happily overlook (and often even enjoy) the occasional controversy or Easter egg.

Remember, this isn't about tricking people. It's about understanding how the game is played. You can either ignore how platforms really work and stay invisible... or lean in, play smart, and grow while still helping people.

A Final Warning

Yes, this strategy attracts trolls. That's the unavoidable cost of visibility in today's social media world. But I've learned after billions of views: the people worth building a business around aren't the ones screaming in your comments.

The right audience, the buyers, the loyal fans, the ones who will ride with you for years, see through the noise. They recognize your value. They stick.

If someone storms off because they're "offended," good. They weren't your customers anyway.

The goal isn't vanity metrics. The goal is the *right* audience, an audience that trusts you, buys from you, and fuels your business. And sometimes? That means being willing to ruffle feathers along the way.

What were your 3 key takeaways:

_____

_____

_____

What 3 additional action steps are you going to take:

_____

_____

_____

What is the deadline you're setting for each of these steps:

_____

_____

_____

Chapter 13: Instagram

Instagram is still one of the most powerful platforms for building a personal brand and turning content into cash. Period.

Whether you're just starting or trying to break through a plateau, this chapter is your blueprint. No vague motivational fluff, just the exact tactical strategies I use and teach creators, coaches, and entrepreneurs every single day.

Here's the truth: people are still treating Instagram like it's 2017. Too many selfies. Overthinking aesthetics. Ignoring the built-in tools that actually move the needle.

But if you commit to what works right now, with clarity, creativity, and boldness, you can cut through the noise and build something real.

1. Hook Them Immediately

After studying and testing thousands of videos, one truth stands out: the winners always have a **powerful hook within the first 2–3 seconds**.

It doesn't matter if it's video or Reels, Instagram is no different. Your opening must grab attention instantly, or the scroll continues without you.

A hook can be **audible** (what you say) or **visual** (what they see). The goal is the same: spark curiosity with something surprising, dramatic, or slightly exaggerated that ties directly to your niche.

Examples of Audible Hooks You Can Steal Today:

- "This Instagram update feels ILLEGAL to know!"

- "Instagram might BAN you if you don't know this hack."

- "You're throwing away followers if you ignore this Instagram trick."

Hooks like these have personally generated **billions of views** for me, and more importantly, they've directly translated into revenue.

Instagram Hook Bank

Universal Hooks (any niche):

1. "This [topic] hack feels ILLEGAL to know."

2. "You might get BANNED if you don't fix this."

3. "You're throwing away [x opportunity] if you ignore this trick."

4. "Most people are doing [x thing] WRONG. Here's how to

fix it."

5. "If I had to start from scratch today, here's exactly what I'd do."

6. "Stop making this ONE mistake [on topic], it's killing your potential [outcome]."

7. "I tested this for 30 days, here's what actually works."

8. "Why nobody is seeing your posts (and how to change it)."

9. "I bet you've never tried this [topic] growth shortcut."

10. "This is the #1 reason your [x topic] isn't performing well."

Coaches / Educators / Consultants

1. "My client went from $3K months to $30K months. Here's the 3-word framework that did it."

2. "You're working 60-hour weeks, but still can't pay yourself a real salary. Here's why."

3. "Your competitors with worse products are outselling you 10-to-1. Here's their secret."

4. "You're undercharging because you're scared they'll say no. Here's what's really happening."

5. "You don't need a huge following to make sales. You need THIS."

Fitness / Health / Wellness

1. "This workout mistake is killing your gains."

2. "You're eating healthy but STILL not losing weight, here's why."

3. "Stop doing this exercise, it's wrecking your back."

4. "The 3 supplements I'd never waste money on again."

5. "If I had to start my fitness journey over, I'd do this first."

E-commerce / Product Brands

1. "You've been lied to about [product type]."

2. "The secret behind why this product keeps selling out."

3. "3 reasons people don't buy your product (and how to fix it)."

4. "This $20 product can save you $200."

5. "Why nobody is buying from your store, and how to change that today."

Real Estate / Local Business

1. "The housing market is about to change. Here's what you need to know."

2. "3 mistakes first-time buyers make (and how to avoid

them)."

3. "This hack could save you thousands on your next home."

4. "Why renting is secretly costing you more than you think."

5. "The one thing your realtor isn't telling you."

AI / Tech / Software

1. "Marketers don't want you to know this ChatGPT hack."

2. "Stack these 3 AI tools together and you'll destroy the internet."

3. "This AI tool will scare you!"

4. "Stop wasting time on Canva, do this instead."

5. "The AI shortcut that just saved me 10 hours."

How to Use This Bank:

- Swap the nouns to fit your niche.

- Keep the tone **surprising, bold, or urgent.**

- Don't be afraid of exaggeration. It's what makes people stop scrolling.

2. Leverage Instagram Reels + Automation (Many-Chat & Go High Level)

Instagram Reels are a very powerful driver of organic reach right now. But here's the kicker: when you combine them with automation tools like **ManyChat** or **Go High Level**, you don't just get views, you turn those views into leads and sales on autopilot.

Here's the exact play:

1. **Post a highly engaging Reel.** Keep it short, clear, and value-packed.

2. **Add a trigger word.** In the video, say something like: "Comment the word *STRATEGY* and I'll DM you the details."

   ◦ Show it as **on-screen text** (subtitles).

   ◦ Make it the **first line in your caption** so it appears above the fold.

   ◦ Repeat it verbally so it sticks. The more visible your trigger, the more comments you'll get.

3. **Automate the response.** Use ManyChat or Go High Level to automatically reply to every comment and send a personalized DM. This DM can include:

   ◦ Extra value (quick tips, resources)

   ◦ A free lead magnet

   ◦ Or a direct offer that moves them down your funnel

4. **Convert conversations into clients.** This one system

has generated me *thousands* of direct messages and turned casual followers into paying customers.

Pro Tip: Comments aren't just engagement. They're a list. Every person who drops your trigger word is raising their hand, saying, *"I'm interested."* Automations let you scale those conversations without burning out in your DMs.

If you're serious about rapid growth on Instagram, **start pairing Reels with automation immediately.** It's one of the highest ROI moves you can make.

DM Automation Script Bank

Script 1: Value Drop (Quick Win)

Trigger word: STRATEGY **DM Sequence:**

1. *"Hey [first name], thanks for commenting STRATEGY As promised, here's the exact 3-step Instagram growth tactic I use with my clients:"*

   - Step 1: [Insert tip]

   - Step 2: [Insert tip]

   - Step 3: [Insert tip]

2. *"Try this today and let me know how it works for you. Want me to send you a deeper breakdown with templates?"*

Script 2: Lead Magnet Delivery

Trigger word: GUIDE **DM Sequence:**

1. *"You got it! Here's your free Instagram Growth Guide: [link]."*

2. *"Inside you'll find 10 strategies that are working right now (step by step). Which one are you most excited to try first?"* *[link].*

3. (If they reply) —> *"Love it. I also teach this in more depth in my program. Want me to send you details?"*

Script 3: Storytelling CTA

Trigger word: GROWTH **DM Sequence:**

"Hey [first name], I saw you commented GROWTH. Quick story: one of my clients was stuck at 2,000 followers for months. We used the framework I just shared, and in 60 days, they jumped to 15K followers + booked 4 new clients."

"Do you want me to send you the exact checklist they used?"

Script 4: Mini-Offer (Soft Sell)

Trigger word: COACHING **DM Sequence:**

"Thanks for dropping COACHING, [first name]. Most people don't know this, but Instagram isn't about posting more. It's about

posting smarter. I break this down for my private coaching clients every week."

"Want me to send you the details on how my coaching works so you can see if it's a fit?"

Script 5: Event/Challenge Promo

Trigger word: CHALLENGE **DM Sequence:**

"You're in! Here are the details for the 5-Day Instagram Challenge starting [date]: [link]."

"During the challenge, I'll show you how to [result] in less than a week. Day 1 is my favorite. Want me to give you a sneak peek?"

Script 6: Upsell from Freebie —> Paid

Trigger word: TIPS **DM Sequence:**

"Here are the 5 quick Instagram tips you asked for: [tip list or link]."

"If you want the full 30-day content calendar I use with clients, I can send you the link. It's a small investment, but it saves you hours. Want it?"

Pro Tip for Readers: Always start with value —> ask permission —> then offer. This feels conversational, not spammy, and keeps trust high.

3. Leverage Instagram Stories with Strategic Formats

Instagram Stories are a highly **underutilized growth tool** on the platform. They're not just "extra content", they're a daily touchpoint that builds trust and keeps you top of mind.

The key? Don't post random updates. Use **strategic formats** that spark engagement and create connection.

Story Formats That Work Right Now:

Polls + Questions

- Simple, direct prompts boost engagement and give you instant market research.

- Example: *"Are you seeing lower reach on Instagram? Yes or No?"*

Behind-the-Scenes

- Share your daily routine, office setup, or how you create content.

- Transparency builds relatability, and relatability builds trust.

Mini-Educational Series

- Use a 3-5 slide Story sequence to break down one tip or tutorial.

- Quick, digestible value = instant credibility.

Share Your Reels to Stories

- Pro tip: Story views count toward your Reel views.

- Add a call-to-action sticker: *"Tap here to watch the full Reel."*

Why This Works:

- Stories humanize your brand.

- They create **micro-engagement** (poll votes, question responses) that tell the algorithm your audience cares about your content.

- They train your audience to check in with you daily, not just when a Reel happens to pop up.

If you want to stay relevant and trustworthy, **show up in Stories as much as you show up in Reels.**

7-Day Instagram Story Plan

Day 1: Poll / Question

- Post a poll or slider sticker related to your niche.

- Example: *"Are you struggling with [your topic]? Yes | No"*

- Goal: Boost engagement + collect insights.

Day 2: Behind-the-Scenes

- Share a look at your day, workspace, or content creation process.

- Example: *"Here's what my setup looks like before filming a Reel"*

- Goal: Build trust + humanize your brand.

Day 3: Mini Tutorial

- Break down one quick tip across 3–5 slides.

- Example: *"3 Hashtag Hacks That Still Work in 2025"*

- Goal: Deliver quick-win value.

Day 4: Reel Reshare

- Share your latest Reel directly into Stories.

- Add a call-to-action sticker: *"Tap to watch"*

- Goal: Boost Reel views + story activity.

Day 5: Client Win / Case Study

- Share a client testimonial, result, or transformation.

- Example: *"One of my students gained 10K followers in 60 days using this."*

- Goal: Social proof + authority.

Day 6: Engagement Sticker

- Use a quiz or emoji slider to spark interaction.

- Example: *"How confident are you with [Topic]? Slide "*

- Goal: Keep people interacting with your content.

Day 7: Personal Connection

- Share something non-business: a hobby, family moment, or personal reflection.

- Example: *"Sunday reset routine "*

- Goal: Relatability + deepen personal connection.

Pro Tip for Readers: Rotate this 7-day cycle weekly —> it gives you variety, keeps engagement high, and ensures your Stories work for value, trust, AND conversions.

4. Use Instagram Carousels for Deeper Education

Carousels are **underrated growth hacks** on Instagram. Why? Because they let you deliver deeper, more structured content, and the algorithm loves them.

Every swipe on a carousel is an **engagement signal**, which means your content stays in feeds longer and reaches more people. Think of carousels as mini-courses your audience can learn from, save, and share.

Carousels Work Best For:

- **Step-by-Step Guides**: Break down a process into clear,

swipeable actions.

- **Tip Lists**: "5 Instagram Growth Hacks You Can Try Today."

- **Before & After Examples**: Show transformation visually (great for fitness, real estate, design).

- **Data-Driven Infographics**: Simplify complex stats or industry insights into snackable slides.

Pro Tip:

- Design the **first slide like a headline** —> it must stop the scroll ("The 3 Mistakes Killing Your Reach").

- Make the **middle slides value-packed** —> each one should stand alone as a micro-lesson.

- End with a **call-to-action slide** —> "Save this for later" or "DM me 'GROWTH' for the full guide." Remember to stack this with ManyChat or Go High Level.

Carousels aren't just posts. They're assets your audience will revisit over and over, positioning you as an authority.

Pro Tips for Readers:

- Use **bold, readable fonts** (think billboard, not fine print).

- Keep text minimal —> one idea per slide.

- First slide = the headline —> if it doesn't grab attention, the rest won't matter.

5. Instagram "Trial Reels" A Massive Hack Right Now

One of my favorite growth strategies on Instagram right now is what I call **"Trial Reels."**

Trial Reels are designed for **rapid experimentation**, testing multiple hooks, formats, and content topics to see what sticks. The goal isn't perfection. It's speed.

The best part? Instagram's Trial Reels setting lets you post to a **brand-new audience that doesn't already follow you.** That means instant market testing with fresh eyes, and huge opportunities to repurpose top performers.

How to Implement Trial Reels

1. Test Different Hooks

- Experiment with bold, surprising, or exaggerated openings relevant to your niche.

- Example: *"This Instagram feature feels ILLEGAL... "* vs. *"Most creators are using this WRONG... "*

2. Rapid Publish

- Post multiple Trial Reels in a single day.

- Focus on quantity over quality. The goal is testing, not perfection.

3. **Evaluate Performance**

- Track analytics (views, watch time, engagement).

- Identify which hooks and formats hit hardest.

4. **Double Down on Winners**

- Push the winning version to your main feed and broader audience.

- Repurpose older viral content: repost a top-performing Reel as a Trial Reel and reach a completely new audience. (I've had videos go viral *several times* using this strategy.)

Why Trial Reels Work

- They cut the guesswork out of content creation.

- They deliver fast clarity on what resonates with your audience.

- They allow you to recycle proven hits for more reach and growth.

Trial Reels = **data-driven growth.** Test fast, find winners, and scale impact.

Track Key Metrics (24 - 48 hrs)

Use this grid to evaluate each Trial Reel:

Reel #	Hook	Views	Watch Time %	Saves	Shares	Comments	Winner?
1	...	...	...	...	...	...	☑ /✗
2	...	...	...	...	...	...	☑ /✗
3	...	...	...	...	...	...	☑ /✗
4	...	...	...	...	...	...	☑ /✗
5	...	...	...	...	...	...	☑ /✗

6. The Power of Instagram Live

Instagram Live is a very powerful tools for building trust because it gives your audience **real-time, unfiltered access** to you. It's raw, personal, and interactive, which makes it one of the deepest connection points on social media.

But going Live isn't about winging it. The successful creators treat Lives like mini-events.

A personal example, when we launched my company, Syllaby, on , I had one goal: to be the number 1 product of the day. What did I do? I live-streamed on IG for 8 hours straight. I changed the link in my bio directly to our ProductHunt link so that everyone could vote, and for 8 hours straight, I was giving free, actionable advice, building rapport, and bringing attention to our campaign.

Results? It worked. We were the number 1 product of the day, resulting in 1000s of website visitors and 100s of signups.

Proven Instagram Live Strategies:

Live Q&As

- Invite your audience to ask anything about your niche, business, or even your personal journey.

- Example: *"Drop your questions about [your topic] in the chat, I'll answer live!"*

Interviews + Collaborations

- Go Live with influencers, clients, or peers.

- Cross-pollinate audiences and instantly double your reach.

Product or Service Demonstrations

- Show, don't just tell.

- Example: Live walkthroughs of how your product/service works, client transformations, or a tutorial of your service in action.

Pro Tips for Lives:

- **Promote ahead of time:** Announce the Live on Stories

and feed posts so people plan to join.

- **Engage early:** Greet viewers by name as they join, which keeps them in the room longer.

- **Call-to-action:** End every Live with a next step: "DM me 'LIVE' for the full resource," "Grab my free guide in the link," or "Follow for weekly Lives."

- **Repurpose:** Save the Live replay and chop it into Reels or Carousels for extended shelf life.

Instagram Live = instant trust-building, amplified reach, and content you can repurpose for weeks.

Instagram Live Event Framework

Pre-Live Prep Checklist

- **Topic:** Choose 1 clear topic (Ex: *"3 Hacks to Double Your Reach on Instagram"*).

- **Promotion:** Announce on Stories & feed 24 hours before + reminder 1 hour before.

- **CTA Plan:** Decide the call-to-action before you go live (DM keyword, freebie, product/service).

- **Environment:** Quiet, well-lit space + stable internet.

- **Tools:** Notes or bullet points handy, water nearby.

30-Minute Live Flow Script

Minute 0–2 —> Welcome & Energy

- Greet new viewers by name as they join.

- Example: *"Hey [name], glad you're here! Drop in the chat where you're watching from."*

- Share topic upfront: *"Today I'm breaking down 3 simple hacks to double your Instagram reach."*

Minute 3 - 10 —> Deliver Quick Wins

- Teach 1–2 value-packed tips right away.

- Keep it interactive —> "Comment YES if you've ever struggled with this."

- Use visual aids (screen share, product demo, props).

Minute 11 - 20 —> Deep Dive / Showcase

- Expand with examples, case studies, or step-by-step walk-throughs.

- If collaborating, ask your guest engaging questions.

- Share a story that humanizes you (behind-the-scenes, client success).

Minute 21 - 25 —> Engage & Q&A

- Answer audience questions live.

- Example: *"Drop your biggest [topic] challenge below and I'll answer right now."*

Minute 26 - 30 —> Call-to-Action + Close

- Give a clear next step:

  - "DM me the word *GROWTH* for my free guide."

  - "Follow for more weekly tips."

  - "Check the link in bio to grab the full playbook."

- End with gratitude + teaser for the next Live.

- Save the replay —> repurpose clips into Reels, Stories, Carousels.

Pro Tip for Readers: Treat every Live like a **mini-webinar.** Give so much value that people think, *"If this is free, the paid stuff must be insane."*

8. Collaborate With Similar Creators

Instagram's **collaboration feature** is one of the fastest ways to grow right now. Whether it's a Reel, Image, or Carousel, you can add up to **5 collaborators,** and when you do, that post goes out to **all of your audiences at once.**

That means your content gets instant exposure to entirely new communities without running ads. The more you collaborate, the faster you grow.

How to Put Collabs Into Play

1. Identify Similar Creators

- Look for people in your niche with complementary expertise.

- Example: A fitness trainer collabs with another fitness trainer or a nutrition coach.

2. Form a Collab Group

- Be the leader. Create a DM group with similar creators in your space.

- Message template you can use: *"Hi [name]! I'm in your niche, and I'm organizing a group for collabs. We can all help each other grow by adding one another as collaborators on Reels, Carousels, or posts. Want in?"*

3. Rotate Collaborators

- Switch up who you tag each time so everyone gets exposure.

- Keep it fresh by doing solo collabs, group collabs, and occasional themed content.

4. Leverage the Algorithm

- Collab posts often get boosted by Instagram because they drive **cross-audience engagement.**

- Bonus: More comments, shares, and saves across multiple accounts = stronger reach for everyone.

Pro Tip: Don't just collab with peers, think bigger. Bring in influencers, clients, or even brands. Their audiences will instantly associate you with authority and credibility.

Collabs aren't just growth hacks, they're **relationship builders.** And relationships drive long-term success on Instagram.

Instagram Collab Playbook

10 Ready-Made Collab Content Ideas

1. **Tip Swap Reel**: Each creator shares one quick tip in a single Reel.

   - Title: *"5 Experts Share Their Best Instagram Growth Hack"*

2. **Before & After Carousel**: Each creator shows a transformation (fitness, business, real estate, design).

3. **Challenge Series**: *"5 Days to [Result]"* —> each creator posts a daily tip or action step.

4. **Myth-Busting Reel**: Each person debunks a common myth in their niche.

   - Example: *"Stop believing this Instagram myth..."*

5. **Joint Tutorial**: Creator A explains Step 1, Creator B explains Step 2, and so on.

6. **Case Study Collab**: Share a client/student transformation together (coach + service provider).

7. **Bonus Offer Stacking:** You can earn affiliate commissions for sales together by stacking bonus offers and everyone collaborating on that post.

8. **Roundtable Live**: Host a multi-person Instagram Live, then repurpose clips as Reels.

9. **Tool Stack Post**: Each creator shares their favorite app/tool —> carousel titled *"6 Tools We Can't Live Without."*

10. **"What I'd Do If I Started Over" Reel**: Each creator gives one piece of advice for beginners in their niche.

DM Templates for Starting Collabs

Initial Outreach:

"Hey [Name]! I've been following your content and love what you're doing in [niche]. I'm organizing a small collab group where we help each other grow by adding one another as collaborators on posts. Totally free, just creators supporting creators. Want in?"

Group Invite:

"Hi everyone! Excited to kick off this collab group Here's the idea: we'll rotate collabs (Reels, Carousels, Lives) so we all tap into each other's audiences. Drop your best content ideas here and let's start scheduling."

Collab Confirmation:

"Hey [Name], thanks for jumping in! For our first collab, how about we do a [tip swap / myth-busting Reel / joint carousel]? I'll draft an outline and tag you as a collaborator when I post."

Pro Tip for Readers: Don't overthink collabs. Even a simple two-person Reel can double your reach. The key is consistency. Treat collabs like part of your monthly content strategy, not a one-off.

Your Next Step

If you remember nothing else from this chapter, remember this: **Instagram rewards clarity, creativity, and consistency.**

Don't overcomplicate it. Don't wait for the "perfect" strategy. Perfection kills momentum.

Pick just **two of the strategies** you learned here, whether it's Reels + automation, collabs, or carousels, and put them into play this week.

Your blueprint is here. The only thing standing between you and growth is action.

Cut through the noise. Start today.

What were your 3 key takeaways:

_____

_____

_____

What 3 additional action steps are you going to take:

_____

_____

_____

What is the deadline you're setting for each of these steps:

_____

_____

_____

Chapter 14: Facebook

Look, I don't care what your opinion on Facebook is. Maybe you think it's not the sexiest platform out there. Maybe you think it's where your parents hang out, posting baby pictures and minion memes. I get it.

But here's the brutal truth: if you're creating content and you're not active on Facebook right now, you're **literally leaving money on the table.**

The organic reach on this platform is absolutely insane. And the payouts? They'll make your jaw drop. In the last 30 days alone, I've driven hundreds of millions of views, gained hundreds of thousands of new followers, and cashed five figures in direct Facebook payouts, not even counting the leads, email sign-ups, and sales that come with it.

In this chapter, I'm going to pull back the curtain on exactly how I'm doing it. You'll see my analytics, the posts that are working best right now, and the daily strategy you can copy and adapt for your business.

Facebook isn't dead. It's the sleeping giant of social media that just woke up. And if you're smart enough to act now, you can ride this wave while most people are still sleeping on it.

Why Facebook is My #1 Platform (And Should Be Yours Too)

Right now, Facebook is hands down my number one organic platform across all of social media. I've built over **2 million followers** here, and every single one came from organic strategies. No ads. No fake followers. Just pure consistency and smart execution.

Now, let me blow your mind with some numbers. In just the last 28 days, I pulled in:

- **300 million views**

- **200,000 new followers**

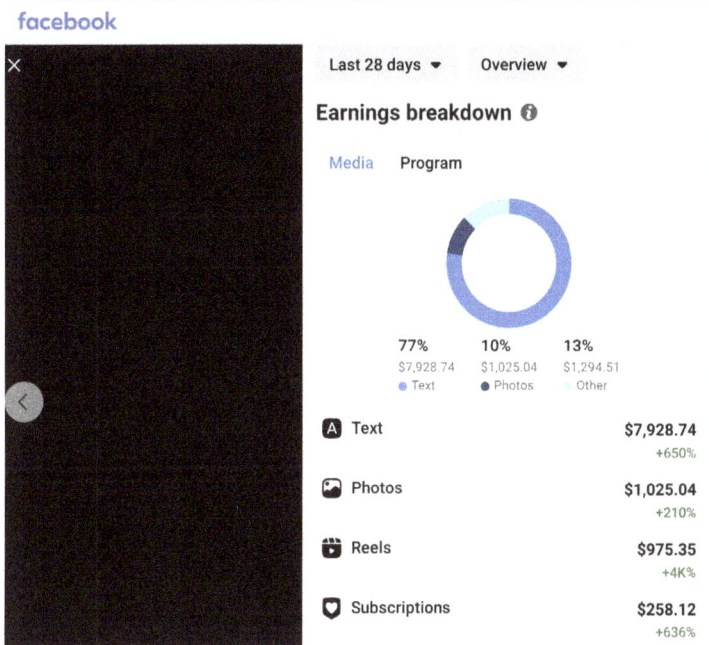

facebook

Last 28 days ▼   Overview ▼

Earnings breakdown ⓘ

Media   Program

	77%	10%	13%
	$7,928.74	$1,025.04	$1,294.51
	● Text	● Photos	Other

🅐 Text	$7,928.74
	+650%
🖼 Photos	$1,025.04
	+210%
▶ Reels	$975.35
	+4K%
🛡 Subscriptions	$258.12
	+636%

And here's the kicker: **77% of those views came from text-based content.** Not videos. Not fancy graphics. Simple text posts, threads, and memes are driving the majority of my massive reach.

And Facebook is paying out big for this content. Individual posts have earned me anywhere from **$1 to $1,500 each.** That's before factoring in affiliate commissions, product sales, and cross-platform growth.

But here's the real secret: the **direct payout is just the tip of the iceberg.** The real money comes from what Facebook drives *beyond Facebook*. Every time one of my posts goes viral, I see:

- A spike in **email sign-ups**

- A surge in **YouTube views**

- More **product sales**

- More **affiliate commissions**

- Extra **conference ticket sales**

Facebook is my hub. It feeds every other channel, every offer, every piece of my business. That's why it's my #1 platform, and if you're serious about growth, it should be yours too. Keep people curious enough to dive into the comments.

That simple format is what's driving the majority of my reach right now. Photo-oriented content comes in second. And here's the part that blows most people's minds: **Facebook Reels only account for 0.7% of my content performance.**

Yes, less than 1%. While everyone else is burning out chasing the perfect Reel, I'm over here stacking millions of views (and payouts) with simple text posts.

The real magic isn't just the post itself. It's the format. Use a bold **colored background for the hook**, then stack the rest of your content in the **comments below.** Facebook's comment system is messy; threads get jumbled and buried. That means when people go digging for the tips you promised, they **engage more** because they don't know to sort comments "by all" instead of recommended, which Facebook defaults to. For this reason, they comment, asking where number X and number Y are. The algorithm reads that as quality content, and your reach skyrockets.

Real Examples, Real Numbers

Let me back this up with some concrete examples so you know I'm not just blowing smoke.

I posted a simple text thread about how airlines should be afraid of ChatGPT because I found a flight trick that saved me over $1,000. Straightforward idea, valuable info, written conversationally.

The results?

- **8,100 engagements**

- **700 comments**

- **4,000 shares**

- **8.4 million reach**

- **$440 payout from Facebook**

For a post that, believe it or not, **AI wrote in less than a minute.**

Here's another one: a plain text post. No fancy design. No video editing. It pulled in:

- **16,000 likes**

- **937 comments**

- **8500 shares**

- **21 million reach**

- **$988 payout**

Austin Armstrong ✓
July 27 · 🌐

My friend applied to 57 jobs.
Ghosted 57 times.
Not a single call.

Then I gave ChatGPT his résumé...

7 replies in 6 days.
No fluff. Just better prompts.

Here's exactly what we used:

1. "Act like a recruiter in [industry]. What's missing from this résumé that would stop you from reaching out?"
→ Blind spots exposed in 30 seconds.

2. "Rewrite my résumé summary to feel confident, clear, and tailored to this job: [paste job description]."
→ Specific > impressive. Targeted always wins.

3. "Turn these bullet points into achievement-focused statements — add metrics wherever possible."
→ Buzzwords don't sell. Results do.

4. "Help me reframe a 2-year career gap as growth, not failure."
→ You don't hide it. You own it.

5. "Add ATS keywords from this job post — without sounding robotic."
→ Speak human. Pass robots.

6. "Format this résumé so it's easy to scan, clean to read, and works on any system."
→ No Canva fluff. Just recruiter-ready clarity.

7. "Write a short, punchy message I can DM a hiring manager — no desperation, just value."
→ Because standing out starts before the résumé.

It wasn't the economy.
It was the strategy.

Use better prompts.
Get better results.

👍❤️ Mike Cavaggioni, Afarin G Somers and 16K others   937 comments   8.5K shares

👍 Like   💬 Comment   ↪ Share

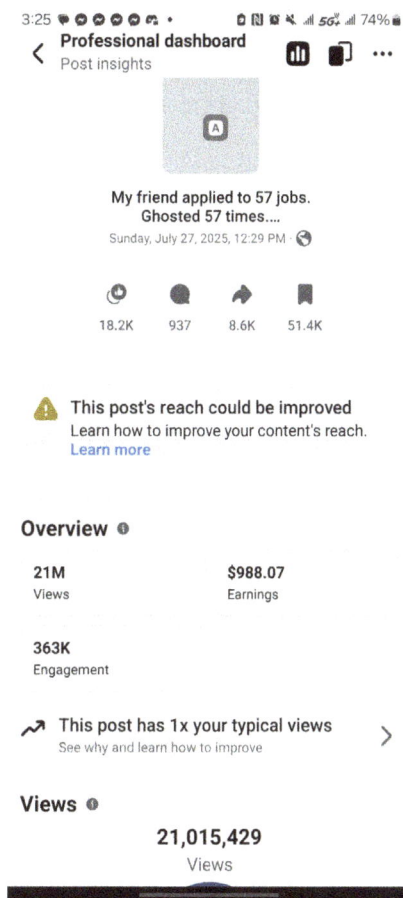

And let me be clear, these aren't one-off lucky breaks. This is my **daily reality.**

The pattern is crystal clear: **text threads are astronomically outperforming everything else on Facebook right now.**

Focus on **value** + **virality** in the headline. Think of it like a magazine cover. If the hook makes people stop and say, "Wait, what?", you've already won.

The Text Thread Formula That Prints Money

Here's my secret sauce, and I'm giving it to you completely free because I believe in lifting others up. This is the exact system that makes text threads my #1 content format on Facebook.

1. The Visual Hook Use Facebook's built-in colored backgrounds. Black background with white text is my personal favorite because it takes up the most real estate in the feed and pops against the endless scroll. Keep the text short, bold, and curiosity-driven, think magazine cover headline.

2. The Tease Always end the main post with downward-pointing finger emojis (). This directs people to the comments where the *real value* lives. It's a subtle curiosity gap that gets people clicking deeper.

3. The Comment Stack Strategy This is where the magic happens. Unlike the previous screenshot examples, this is a second text-based strategy where you break down each individual tip into one comment at a time.

- Facebook's comment system is chaotic: comments often get out of order, are buried, and are hard to follow.

- That chaos works in your favor. Readers scroll, search, and even ask, "Where's the info?" Every action equals more engagement.

- More engagement = Facebook assumes it's quality content = more reach.

4. The Call to Action (CTA) Every thread should capture the momentum. In the final comment, I drop a CTA:

- Link to my **email list**

- Direct to my **YouTube channel**

- Or plug an **affiliate tool or product**

Every viral post becomes more than just vanity metrics; it becomes a funnel for your business or a revenue-generating stream.

Rotate your CTAs so you're not always pushing the same thing. One day it's your newsletter, the next it's your YouTube, the next it's an affiliate tool. That way, you're growing multiple assets at once.

Pro Tip: On my phone, in notes, I have at least five or six different call to actions. This is my workflow, so I can easily just copy one after each post.

How AI Can Automate All of This For You

One of the craziest parts of my Facebook strategy is this: **AI, specifically ChatGPT, was writing a lot of my viral threads.**

I'm not exaggerating when I say ChatGPT was literally **printing money** for me on my monetized Facebook profile. I fed it the right structure, it gave me high-performing threads, and those threads translated into millions of views and thousands of dollars in payouts.

And here's the kicker: **you can do this too.**

At first, I was prompting ChatGPT manually every single time, writing detailed instructions, pasting examples, and tweaking the output. It worked, but it was clunky and time-consuming.

Then came ChatGPT Tasks, which was a feature that let me automate it every day, inside ChatGPT, but it still took a lot of time, didn't have my past best performing examples, and a couple of other little nuances that annoyed me.

So, I made it easier. I Vibecoded a tool called ThreadMaster.ai that automates the entire process. You just type in a topic, and it instantly generates a viral-style text thread in the exact format I use every day. I also indexed all of my top-performing, previous threads, so I could easily access them at any given time. And I care so much about helping you succeed that I made this tool public for only $5 per month. No prompt engineering. No wasted time. Just plug, post, and profit.

AI isn't replacing creators, it's giving us leverage. Instead of spending hours writing content, you can generate it in minutes and focus on what actually drives revenue: engagement, community, and smart CTAs.

P.S. Towards the end of this book, I have dedicated a chapter to how you can Vibecode your own tools.

In Case You're Curious About ThreadMaster.ai

It has four core features that will transform your Facebook game:

1. AI Thread Generator: Type in any topic, "new homeowner hacks" if you're in real estate, "ChatGPT hacks" if you're in AI, "fitness myths" if you're in health, and it instantly generates a complete viral-style text thread (like the examples I showed earlier). The AI handles the content creation. All you need to do is copy & paste.

2. Proven Templates: I loaded my **top-performing thread structures** directly into ThreadMaster. These aren't random ideas. These are threads that have generated **millions of views**

and thousands of dollars in revenue. You can swipe, adapt, and make them your own.

3. Viral Image Library: I've indexed over **100 of the most viral images** on Facebook, quote cards, motivational visuals, trending memes, you name it. All tested, all proven. You can preview and download any of them instantly.

4. Indexed Group You Can Share Into: What I wanted to make sure about ThreadMaster is that anyone can use it, even if you don't have a following. I indexed over 40 Facebook Groups that you can join that allow you to share your content into, to expand your reach.

Pro Tip: The groups that are indexed are general. I would suggest searching on Facebook for groups specific to your niche, joining 10-20 of them, and once a day, sharing these posts into those groups from your page or profile to help you grow faster, even if you're starting from zero.

My Exact 5-Minute Workflow With ThreadMaster .ai

1. **Pick a topic:** e.g., "ChatGPT hacks."

2. **Generate a thread:** ThreadMaster creates a complete post with tips and insights.

3. **Post the hook:** Copy the first line into Facebook with a **colored background** (black + white text stands out best).

4. **Stack the value in comments:** Paste the tips one by one below the post.

5. **Boost reach:** Share the post in **5-10 relevant groups** for exponential visibility.

That's it. The entire process takes **about 5 minutes**, and the result is content that consistently reaches **millions of people** and drives revenue through payouts, leads, and sales.

Don't just use the AI as-is. Add your voice, your examples, your credibility. That's what turns "AI-generated" into "audience-resonating."

Pro Tip: This tip will blow your mind: If you have a pro ChatGPT account, you can use ChatGPT agent mode to 1) log into your Facebook page for you, 2) log into your ThreadMaster account, 3) automatically generate your threads as you want in ThreadMaster, and 4) schedule them ahead of time, including the comments. This is literally brand new, the five-minute strategy I just shared above, ChatGPT can completely automate for you.

Proof This System Works (Even for Complete Beginners)

I know what you might be thinking: *"Sure, Austin, this works for you because you already have 2 million followers."*

Fair question. So let me show you what happens when I start from scratch.

Just one week ago, I created a **brand new Facebook page**. Zero followers. Zero analytics. A completely fresh start.

Using only ThreadMaster and my other tools, here's what happened in the first 14 days:

- **883,156 views**

- **779 new followers**

That's the power of this system. It works whether you have **2 million followers or starting with 2.**

You don't need an established audience to see results. What matters is following the formula, creating high-engagement posts, stacking comments for curiosity, and sharing in groups for reach.

Insights

Learn how your Page is performing.

👁
883,156 ↑ 100%
Views ⓘ

💬
4 ↑ 100%
Messaging conversations star ⓘ

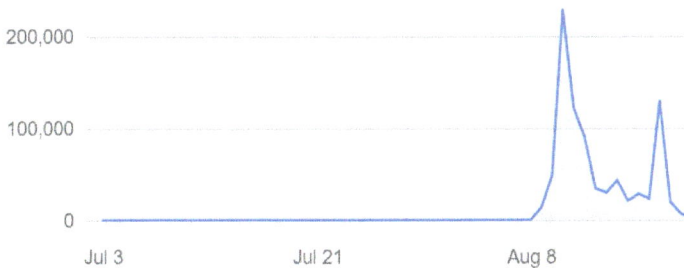

Advanced Strategies That Amplify Everything

The Group Game

Remember the old-school Facebook strategy of joining groups? Guess what, **it still works, and it works better than ever.**

Here's what I do: I regularly search for groups related to AI, marketing, business, or whatever niche I'm posting in. Once I find them, I share my best-performing content into **5–10 relevant groups.**

Important: This is not spam if you do it right. These groups are hungry for quality content. If your post is genuinely helpful, it gets engagement, starts conversations, and can even go viral inside those communities.

Always engage in the group outside of your posts. Comment on other people's threads, answer questions, and build rapport. When you finally drop your content, it feels like value from a trusted member, not a random drive-by.

Broadcast Channels

If you have access to Facebook's **broadcast channel feature**, use it religiously. Think of it like your own personal megaphone: a **one-way communication channel** where your audience can see and react to your posts, but can't flood you with comments.

The engagement rates are ridiculous. For example, I promoted a single YouTube video to my broadcast channel. With **12,800 members**, that post reached **4,500 people.** That's an insane reach-to-subscriber ratio you won't find anywhere else.

And the possibilities are endless:

- Cross-promote your **YouTube videos** or podcasts

- Share **affiliate links** directly with a warm audience

- Drive traffic to **courses, offers, or events**

- Drop quick **exclusive tips** to boost your authority

Theme your channel around a specific promise. Mine is *"Austin's AI Tips."* That way, people know exactly what they're signing up for, and they stick around because the value stays consistent.

Collaboration Pods

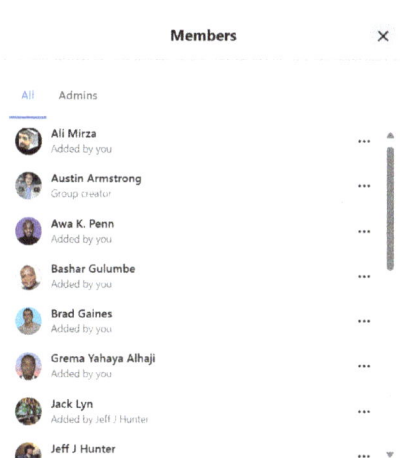

Members ✕

All   Admins

Ali Mirza
Added by you

Austin Armstrong
Group creator

Awa K. Penn
Added by you

Bashar Gulumbe
Added by you

Brad Gaines
Added by you

Grema Yahaya Alhaji
Added by you

Jack Lyn
Added by Jeff J Hunter

Jeff J Hunter

Here's a strategy most people never even think of: I organized a **private group chat with about 10 other AI content creators** in my niche.

Every single day, each of us shares one of our **top-performing posts** in the chat. Everyone else in the group then shares it with their own audience.

The result?

- I don't have to create 10 original posts a day.

- My content gets amplified to 10x the audience.

- Their content gets amplified by me and the rest of the group.

It's not fake. It's not manipulative. We're all providing genuine value to audiences with overlapping interests.

The secret is simple: **collaboration beats competition every single time.**

As the proverb says:

"If you want to go fast, go alone. If you want to go far, go together."

This single strategy helps me **maintain my 10-20 posts/day cadence** without burning out. More importantly, it strengthens relationships with other creators. We're not just sharing posts, we're sharing insights, solving problems, and lifting each other up.

Start small. Identify 3-5 peers in your niche and invite them to a collab chat. Over time, expand to 10+. The more aligned the group is, the stronger the amplification effect.

My favorite part about this whole journey? **My people.**

We call ourselves *The AI Goon Squad.* What started as a simple online group chat turned into a real-world powerhouse of creators, builders, and marketers who genuinely want to see each other win.

We've met up in person multiple times, at conferences, masterminds, and live events across the country. We don't just collaborate online; we strategize together, celebrate together, and push each other to the next level.

As a group, we've:

- **Won affiliate competitions**

- **Landed brand deals and speaking opportunities**

- **Cross-promoted each other's offers, launches, and projects**

- **Referred clients and business back and forth**

It's proof that when you surround yourself with the right people, growth happens faster, and it happens together.

Collaboration isn't just a strategy; it's a multiplier. The faster you find your version of the "Goon Squad," the faster everything changes.

The Volume Game (And Why Most People Fail)

Here's something most people don't want to hear: I recommend you post a **minimum of 5-10 times every single day** on Facebook. I personally post 10-20 posts every single day.

Sounds insane, right? But this volume is exactly what's driving my results.

This strategy is going to piss a lot of "gurus" off. I believe that quantity over quality is where you should focus first, because quantity leads to quality. And let's be clear, this isn't about spamming garbage posts just to hit a quota. It's about posting **valuable content consistently** and letting the data show you what resonates. The more you post, the faster you learn what works, and the faster the algorithm learns who to show your content to.

Here's how I hit that volume without burning out:

- **Original content** I create myself (text threads, memes, and short & long form videos).

- **Collaboration pods** (my peers share mine, I share theirs).

- **Repurposed content:** your Facebook memories act as a great place to find content that you can repurpose. Every day, I look at my memories and look for evergreen content I can post today.

Don't think of it as 10 brand-new pieces of content every day. Think of it as a mix: 2-3 originals, 3-4 collab shares, 1-2 repurposed pieces. Suddenly, "volume" isn't crazy, it's a system.

Cross-Platform Domination

One of the smartest ways to leverage the virality and organic reach of Facebook is to **drive traffic to your other social media platforms.**

Here's a perfect example: I once created a Facebook thread titled *"Canva is now inside ChatGPT. Here's a step-by-step tutorial."* That simple text post exploded, reaching over **25 million** people.

So, I asked myself, "Why not repurpose this for YouTube?" I remade the exact same piece of content as a short tutorial video using the same headline. But instead of adding the steps in the comments like on Facebook, I linked to the full YouTube video.

That one decision drove almost **90,000 views, several thousand new subscribers, and more than $1,200 in revenue.**

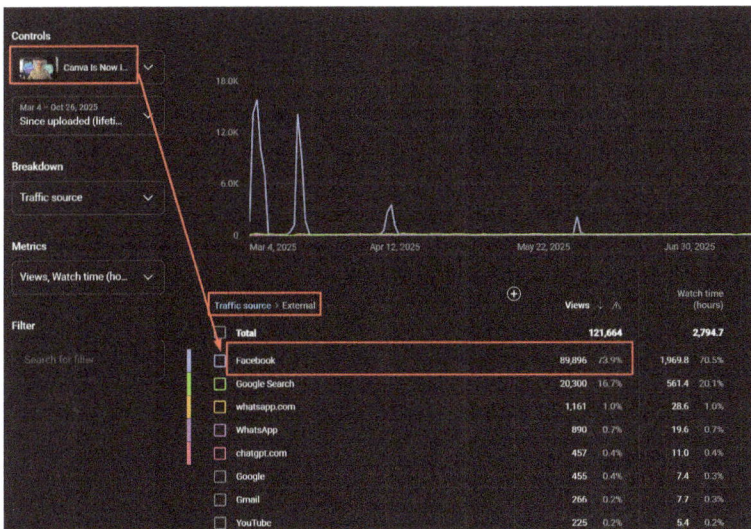

Here's another example. I posted: *"LinkedIn is a free university. But most people don't know. Here are 6 profiles that will teach you more skills than college."* In the comments, I linked to each of those profiles, one per comment, including my own.

I've done this across every platform, **YouTube, LinkedIn, X (Twitter), Threads, and Instagram.** It's one of the best ways to use your free Facebook traffic to grow every other part of your ecosystem.

There's also a deeper layer to this strategy, one that turns growth into community.

I'm a firm believer in lifting others as you rise. There's a well-known African proverb that I use a lot, which says:

"If you want to go fast, go alone. If you want to go far, go together."

When you tag or mention other creators, highlight their work, and genuinely uplift others, something powerful happens: **the law of reciprocity**.

People you tag often reshare your post because it helps them, too. Sometimes, they even create new posts mentioning you in return. That's how collaboration compounds: your audience grows, theirs grows, and everyone wins together.

Cross-platform growth isn't just about algorithms. It's about building relationships, creating value, and using your platforms to amplify others as much as yourself. Everyone grows and everyone wins together.

Your 4-Week Action Plan to Crush Facebook

Ready to stop lurking and start dominating? Here's the exact roadmap I'd follow if I were starting from scratch today:

Week 1: Build Your Foundation

- If you want to use your personal profile, make sure you go into settings and switch it to "professional mode" if you haven't already.

- Optimize your Facebook page or profile around your niche (profile pic, banner, bio).

- Sign up for **ThreadMaster.ai** ($4.99/month, cancel anytime).

- Join **10-20 relevant Facebook groups** in your industry.

Week 2: Launch Your Content System

- Use ThreadMaster to generate your first **10 viral-style text threads.**

- Post **3-5 times per day** using the colored background + comment stack formula.

- Share your best posts into groups for extra reach.

- Connect with and follow 5-10 of the top creators in your niche and naturally engage with their content every day.

- Track what's working, hooks, topics, and formats.

Week 3: Amplify Your Reach

- Set up a **Broadcast Channel** (if available).

- Build your **Collaboration Pod** (DM 5-10 peers and form a repost chat).

- Increase posting volume to **5-10 times/day.**

- Test **viral images** from ThreadMaster's library.

Week 4: Optimize & Scale

- Analyze your top-performing content for **repeatable patterns.**

- Double down on what's working, ditch what's not.

- Start **monetizing your reach** with affiliate links, email list CTAs, or product offers in the comment section of every post.

Don't wait until everything is "perfect." The winners will only reveal themselves once you're in motion. Volume creates clarity. Consistency builds momentum. The only way you will fail is if you quit.

The Bottom Line

Facebook isn't sexy. It's not the shiny new platform everyone's hyping. But you know what it is? **Profitable.** It's where the reach is. It's where the money is. It's where real networking happens. I can't tell you how many doors have opened from Facebook because that's where my network is. It's where we all hang out in between going to conferences and seeing each other in the real world.

While everyone else chases the latest trend, you'll be stacking real wealth and building a real audience on a platform that:

- Actually **pays creators**

- Offers **insane organic reach**

- Can fuel growth across every other channel you own

The opportunity is sitting right in front of you. I've handed you the blueprint, the tools, and the strategies.

The only question is: are you going to take action, or keep making excuses about why Facebook "isn't cool"?

Stop worrying about what's cool. Start focusing on what's **profitable.**

Facebook is wide awake, and it's ready to pay you. **The question is: are you ready to get paid?**

What were your 3 key takeaways:

_____

_____

_____

What 3 additional action steps are you going to take:

_____

_____

_____

What is the deadline you're setting for each of these steps:

_____

_____

Chapter 15: Threads

Let's be real: Threads is a Twitter copycat. They looked at X (formerly Twitter) and said, *"We can build that too."* Classic Meta move.

But here's what most creators miss: copycat or not, Threads has **over 400 million active users**. (At least that's what they're reporting). That's too big to ignore, even if it still feels like Twitter's awkward little brother.

Launched on **July 5, 2023**, Threads is still one of the youngest major social platforms. More than two years in, it's still figuring out what it wants to be. But that uncertainty? That's **your opportunity.** When a platform is still shaping its identity, the algorithm is generous, organic reach is wide open, and the people who experiment early often become the ones who dominate later.

Why You Should Care About Threads

Here's why it matters: **Meta is behind it.** And if history tells us anything, it's that Meta doesn't play around. They have a proven track record of throwing massive resources into making their platforms succeed (remember when people thought Instagram Stories would flop?). If Meta wants Threads to win, they'll find a way to make it win, and the creators who establish themselves early will benefit the most.

Some of the best advice I ever heard in the social media landscape is when a new platform comes out, just grab your @username branded handle a while. Even if you don't want to be super active on the platform, it might take off later, and when you are ready to form a more comprehensive strategy, you will always have your consistent brand @username ready to go.

The Instagram Connection Strategy

Here's your first hack: **connect Threads to your most popular Instagram account.** This isn't optional, it's your fastest growth strategy.

When you create your Threads profile, you're automatically prompted to follow everyone you already follow on Instagram. And the reverse is true: your Instagram followers get nudged to follow you on Threads. That means you're not starting from zero. The platform literally does the audience-building for you.

Here's proof: I have about **840,000 followers on Instagram**, and because of that automatic connection, I have **160,000 followers on Threads**, without having to grind from scratch.

If you don't have a strong Instagram presence yet, focus there first. **Your Instagram growth directly feeds your Threads growth.** Everything compounds.

My Honest Current Threads Strategy: Dump and Test

My strategy? **Dump and test.** Treat Threads as your personal content lab. Don't overthink, don't over-edit, just throw everything at it and see what sticks.

Here's what that looks like in practice:

- **Facebook-style text threads?** Perfect for Threads.

- **Twitter/X-style threads?** Copy, paste, and post.

- **Short-form videos from TikTok, YouTube shorts, or Instagram?** Upload them directly.

- **Memes and images?** Absolutely, they're crushing on Threads right now.

Threads supports almost every content format, so use that flexibility. Think of it as your sandbox: post broadly, post often, and let the algorithm tell you what your audience wants.

What's Actually Working on Threads

After testing different formats, here's what consistently performs best on Threads right now, at least for me:

- **Text Threads (No Surprise):** Just like on Facebook, text-based content dominates. Use the same proven formula, hook, value-packed points, and a clear call to action.

- **Short-Form Videos:** The same content you're posting to TikTok and Instagram Reels works here too. Repurpose, don't reinvent.

- **Conversation Starters:** Threads has a more intimate feel than X/Twitter. Ask questions, spark debates, or invite opinions; people love engaging here.

- **Behind-the-Scenes Content:** Authentic, personal posts resonate. Share glimpses of your process, daily life, or "work in progress" moments to build connection.

The bottom line? **Threads rewards authenticity and experimentation.** Mix these formats and you'll find your sweet spot faster than most creators even realize the opportunity is there. Right now, I think that this is the platform for early adopters. The market hasn't decided what Threads is yet, but it's undeniable that there's a large user base looking and a lack of people creating.

Unique Features to Leverage

Threads isn't just a Twitter / X clone. It has features that can give you an edge if you use them strategically:

- **The Fediverse:** Threads connects to the Fediverse, a network of decentralized platforms that can talk to each other. Most creators ignore this because they don't understand it, but early adopters who learn how to leverage cross-platform communication will stand out.

socialtypro ✔ ⊚ 08/09/25

Don't open this, it might be dangerously helpful:

socialtypro ✔ ⊚ 08/09/25

Don't open this, it might be dangerously helpful:

1. ChatGPT.com → Solve anything
2. Syllaby.io → Create faceless videos
3. Fastread.io → Create ebooks
4. Pika.art → Create videos
5. Gamma.app → Design docs
6. Suno.ai → Make music
7. Bibley.io → AI for the Bible
8. Perplexity.ai → Research assistant
9. Krea.ai → Logo design
10. Fliki.ai → Voiceovers
11. Runway.ml → Film editing
12. Relume.io → Web design
13. LumaLabs.ai → 3D models
14. Descript.com → Edit audio
15. ElevenLabs.io → Clone voices

- **Spoiler Tags:** Highlight text, mark it as a spoiler, and it hides behind a clickable cover. This is a perfect engagement hack. Example: "The #1 AI tool making me $20K/mo is... [Spoiler]." People *have* to click to satisfy their curiosity.

- **Built-In Analytics:** Threads provides native metrics on views, followers, and engagement. Don't just glance at them, track patterns. Double down on content formats and topics that consistently perform best.

- **Cross-Post from Instagram:** A native feature now within Instagram allows you, with a single toggle, to automatically share any or all of your posts directly to Threads.

- **Add Topic:** Rather than a traditional hashtag strategy, you can add a single topic to every given post. This will index that post to interested parties who are interested in that particular topic. For example, almost all of my posts have the "AI" topic.

Most creators don't even realize these features exist, let alone use them. If you do, you'll instantly separate yourself from 90% of the platform.

The Conversation Strategy

Threads isn't about shouting into the void. It's about showing up and talking *with* people. The algorithm rewards real conversations, not one-way broadcasts.

Here's how to make it work:

- **Engage in Your Niche:** Don't just post and disappear. Jump into discussions, reply to creators in your industry, and add value where people are already talking.

- **Consistency = Visibility:** Threads is still small enough that showing up daily gets you noticed fast. Become a familiar voice in your corner of the platform. This is one of those platforms that's easy to become the #1 top creator in your industry, right now.

- **Copy + Remix:** Watch what successful creators in your space are doing. Then put your unique spin on it. Same structure, new voice.

- **Be a Builder, Not a Ghost:** The more you engage, the more the algorithm boosts your reach, and the more opportunities you create for collaborations, partnerships, and growth.

Bottom line: Treat Threads like a networking event, not a billboard. Show up, start conversations, and watch your influence compound.

The Long-Term Threads Play

Here's why I'm bullish on Threads even while it's still figuring itself out: Meta poured billions into Instagram and WhatsApp until they dominated. They'll do the same here.

When Threads eventually locks in its identity and really takes off, and it will, you want to already be established with a content library and a loyal following.

Think about Instagram in 2012, TikTok in 2018, or Facebook in 2008. The early adopters who showed up consistently during the "awkward phase" are the ones with millions of followers and seven-figure businesses today.

Getting in now is planting seeds. When Threads explodes, you'll already have the roots.

Your Threads Action Plan

Week 1: Setup & Connection

- Create your Threads account linked to your strongest Instagram profile (instant follower boost).

- Optimize your bio with keywords + clear value proposition.

- Follow 50 - 100 accounts in your niche to seed your feed.

- Post your first 10 pieces of content (repurposed from Instagram, TikTok, or Facebook).

Week 2: Content Testing

- Post daily using different formats, text threads, videos, memes, images, and conversation starters.

- Engage with 20 - 30 other creators' posts every day.

- Track which formats and hooks earn the most engagement.

Week 3: Community Building

- Join and *start* conversations in your niche.

- Use engagement prompts to spark replies (e.g., "What's one mistake you'll never make again in your business?").

- Collaborate with other creators in your circle, shoutouts, collabs, or repost swaps.

- Lean into your unique Threads "voice" instead of blending in.

Week 4: Optimization & Scale

- Analyze your top-performing posts and identify patterns.

- Double down on what works, cut what doesn't.

- Increase posting frequency if you're seeing momentum.

- Start building deeper relationships with active creators (DMs, collab groups).

Don't Overthink It

This chapter is shorter for a reason. Threads isn't complicated. The strategy is simple:

- Show up

- Post consistently

- Engage genuinely

- Experiment with everything

Threads doesn't have TikTok or YouTube's algorithm complexity. That makes it the perfect playground to build momentum *now*.

Don't wait on the sidelines. Be part of building what Threads becomes.

What were your 3 key takeaways:

_____

_____

_____

What 3 additional action steps are you going to take:

_____

_____

_____

What is the deadline you're setting for each of these steps:

_____

_____

_____

Chapter 16: TikTok

Let's kill the biggest myths right now: It's not a Chinese Trojan Horse. China does not care that you like to watch The Bachelor every Friday in your pajamas. You don't have to dance or lip-sync to win on TikTok. These ideas are outdated, flat-out wrong, and honestly holding people back from the biggest content opportunity of our generation.

In fact, by the time you're reading this, the U.S. will have likely gotten a deal done, so all U.S. operations and TikTok data are controlled by U.S. companies. Get out of your own way and see the opportunity that's right in front of you.

TikTok isn't just an entertainment app. It's a **search engine.** It's a **testing ground.** It's a **money-printing machine.** And if you're not approaching it strategically, you're leaving stacks of cash on the table for someone else.

TikTok as Your Content Testing Lab

TikTok isn't just a place to post. It's your **testing ground.** The platform's algorithm is brutal but brilliant. It gives you almost instant feedback on what hooks work and what flops.

Here's how to use it to your advantage:

Step 1: Keep the core content the same. The body of your video, the lesson, the story, the value, doesn't change. Only the hook does.

Step 2: Test at least three hooks for the same video.

- **Direct Value:** State the benefit upfront. *Example: "5 AI tools that will change your business."*

- **Result Tease:** Tease the outcome before showing how. *Example: "This strategy made me $10K in 30 days."*

- **Negative Hook:** Spark urgency or FOMO. *Example: "Don't do this until you try X" or "The #1 mistake killing your business."*

Step 3: Upload all versions back-to-back. TikTok doesn't punish you for testing. In fact, it thrives on volume. One of those versions will outperform the others.

Step 4: Take the winner and scale it. Once you know which hook works, distribute that version everywhere: YouTube Shorts, Instagram Reels, Facebook Reels, even LinkedIn.

The result? TikTok just ran your market research for free. You didn't guess what would land. You proved it.

The S.T.A.R.T. Framework on TikTok

My S.T.A.R.T. framework works everywhere, but on TikTok, it needs to be sharper and faster. You've got milliseconds to win attention, so here's how to adapt each step:

S - Strong Opening Hook (under 3 seconds) Think of this like a punch in the face (in the best way possible). TikTok users swipe in less than a second if you don't grab them. Your hook should spark curiosity, trigger emotion, or promise instant value. This can be audible or visual.

T - Talk About a Problem Immediately frame the problem your viewer is facing. Create a curiosity gap, make them feel like they can't afford to scroll away until they know the answer.

A - Align with Your Audience Keep this ultra-brief. TikTok isn't YouTube; you don't get 10 seconds to explain yourself. A single line like "If you're a small business owner, this is for you" is enough to show you're speaking directly to them.

R - Resolve with Value Deliver the goods. Give the tip, the hack, the strategy. The more actionable, the better. If they can take what you gave them and use it today, they'll come back tomorrow for more. I mentioned this before, the best marketing strategy I ever learned was to give your best information away for free. Then sell them the implementation.

T - Targeted Call to Action End with one clear direction:

- "Follow for more AI hacks."

- "Comment START and I'll DM you the full guide."

- "Hit the link in bio to grab the checklist."

One CTA, not five. Keep it tight.

Make Your Videos Universally Understandable

If you want to unlock *true* virality, you need to transcend language barriers. Look at Khaby Lame, the most followed person on Tik-Tok. His genius? He doesn't say a single word. His entire brand is built on simple, universally understandable visuals, capped with his signature "this is obviously the better way" gesture.

When your content is visual first, you're no longer limited to English speakers or any one audience. You're speaking to the entire planet. A hack that works in Paris also works in Peru, Lagos, or Tokyo because the message doesn't require translation.

The takeaway: whenever possible, design your content so that it delivers value or entertainment *without relying on words.* Add captions for clarity, but let visuals carry the story. That's how you move from niche recognition to global domination.

TikTok Covers

Most creators hit "publish" without even thinking about their video covers. Huge mistake.

Here's the move: in the first 2 seconds of your video, overlay clear, bold text that works like a clickbait headline. Then, before you publish, set that exact frame as your cover.

What happens? You've just created a custom thumbnail for your TikTok profile. Now, when someone clicks through to your page after watching one of your videos, they don't just see a messy grid of random frames; they see a wall of headlines. Each one tells them exactly what the video is about and why they should watch it.

This instantly makes your profile binge-worthy. People aren't guessing whether a video is worth their time; they *know* from the cover, and they're far more likely to watch multiple videos in one sitting. More views, more followers, more momentum.

The "Perfectionism is Procrastination" Philosophy

TikTok didn't blow up because it was polished. It blew up because it was raw, weird, and unfiltered. That's still what makes it work today.

You don't need ultra-high production quality to win. In fact, over-produced content often feels fake. People crave authenticity.

I'll give you an example: I still record plenty of my videos by literally propping my phone against my laptop and pointing the camera at my screen. No fancy screen-recording software. No expensive gear. Just me, my phone, and the information I want to share.

I'll be blunt: Perfectionism is just procrastination in disguise. Stop waiting until you can afford the perfect setup. You don't need a tripod, a three-point lighting kit, or a $300 microphone. If you've got decent audio and a clear message, you're good to go.

What matters most is the value you deliver and the consistency with which you show up. Your audience will forgive shaky footage, but they won't forgive silence.

So stop obsessing over production value. Start creating. The imperfect video you post today will outperform the "perfect" video you never publish.

The Funnel Strategy: 75-15-5-5

If you want your content to not only reach people but also convert, you need a funnel strategy. Here's the framework I use: **75-15-5-5.**

- **75% Top of Funnel (TOF):** Broad, snackable content that grabs attention and reaches the widest audience. For me, this looks like "useful websites" or "AI tools you need to know." These posts are high-level, instantly digestible, and designed to go viral. Every website that I share would only be used by a business owner, content creator, or aspiring business owner or content creator. All I want to do with Top of Funnel content is to get them aware that I exist and bring them into my ecosystem.

- **15% Middle of Funnel (MOF):** Nurture content that builds trust. Instead of just listing five websites, I'll take one tool and create a step-by-step tutorial showing exactly how to use it. This proves I'm not just curating, I know my stuff.

- **5% Bottom of Funnel (BOF):** Transactional content. This is where you make the ask. Direct sales, limited-time offers, coupon codes, or calls to join your program. For example, I dropped a "50% off Syllaby" coupon recently and brought in 47 new subscribers in just two hours.

- **5% Personal/Behind-the-Scenes:** Don't underestimate this part. Share who you are, what your life looks like, and what drives you. People buy from people they feel connected to.

This is my modern spin on Gary Vaynerchuk's *"Jab, Jab, Jab, Right Hook."* Give value. Give value. Give value. Then ask.

Comment Responses

When a video starts going viral, don't just sit back and watch. **Fan the flames.** The fastest way to do this is by turning comments into content.

Here's why it works:

- **Clickable Path:** When you respond to a comment with a video, the comment itself becomes clickable and links directly back to your original viral post.

- **Content Multiplier:** Each response video creates fresh content with almost no extra effort. Suddenly, one viral video can turn into 10, 20, or even 50 spin-off videos.

- **Virality Fuel:** Every new response funnels traffic back to the original post, extending its lifespan and boosting the algorithm's perception of it.

Think of this like building backlinks in SEO, but for TikTok. Each comment response is an internal link that keeps your viral video in circulation, feeding it more reach, more engagement, and more followers.

Finding Your Series

One of the best hacks that I have found, not only for TikTok but across all social media, is to create a recurrent series that people enjoy. For example, I have multiple series myself, like "These 5 Websites Feel Illegal to Know," "If You Stack These 3 Websites Together..." and "ChatGPT Secrets You Should Know."

The idea here is to have one recurring opening hook, one CTA at the end, but the middle of the video is swappable. Test different opening hooks that could be a series and test each series at least 10 times, to see if people are actually interested or not. One test is not enough. When you find a series that consistently performs well, congratulations, you can scale that almost indefinitely!

This gives people a reason to continue coming back to your channel and can really trigger virality. Having these series has been one of the biggest game changers for me, not only for TikTok but for every social media platform. People have literally looked at me in the streets publicly and said to me, "You're the 5 Websites guy!"

Repost Your Top Performers

Stop falling into the "I need brand-new content every time" trap. That mindset will burn you out, and it's completely unnecessary.

Your best strategy is **reposting your top-performing videos.**

Once a month, I go back through my analytics and pull my winners. Whether they blew up last month, six months ago, or even a year ago, I repost them. Sometimes it's the exact same video, sometimes it's a fresh re-recording of the exact same script. If the content is evergreen, it's still valuable.

Remember this: **you are the only person who sees everything you post.** Most of your audience never saw that video the first time around. The ones who did? They either forgot it or couldn't find it again, and many will thank you for resurfacing it.

Reposting isn't lazy. It's leverage.

Evergreen Content Checklist (Safe to Repost)

- **Timeless Value:** Tips, tools, or strategies that don't expire (e.g., "5 Websites That Save You Money").

- **Repeatable Formats:** Series or list-style content that always performs (e.g., "These X Things Feel Illegal to Know").

- **Inspirational/Motivational Posts:** Quotes, lessons, or mindset shifts that are always relevant.

- **How-To Tutorials:** Step-by-step guides that solve consistent problems.

- **Personal Stories With Lessons:** As long as the takeaway is universal and not tied to a specific date.

Avoid Reposting If:

- It's tied to breaking news or trends that are no longer relevant.

- The product, tool, or platform mentioned no longer works or has changed significantly.

- It includes outdated offers, discounts, or time-sensitive promotions.

TikTok Growth Hacks

1) Comment Hijacking Jump into conversations that already have proven engagement.

- **How:** Find top creators in your niche, scan their most-viewed videos, and look for comments with lots of likes. Record a short reply video addressing that comment (answer the question, expand the idea, or add a contrarian take).

- **Why it works:** You're surfacing in threads where attention is already concentrated, the algorithm notices the connection, and pushes your response.

- **Use sparingly:** Don't spam replies across dozens of creators. One high-quality, genuinely helpful response per day is a good pace. Overdo it and you risk appearing opportunistic or getting blocked by the creator of the video you're doing comment responses to.

- **Pro tip:** Put the original commenter's text on-screen for context and finish with a CTA that links back to your profile content.

2) Hashtag Hijacking Find high-value hashtags that are underserved and own them.

- **How:** Search for relevant hashtags with very high view counts but few recent posts in the feed. Create several short videos using those hashtags so your content eventually sits near the top of that hashtag's results.

- **Why it works:** You're positioning yourself where demand is high and supply is low, an organic shortcut to discoverability.

- **Cadence:** Test 3-5 videos per hashtag over 1-2 weeks and track which hashtags convert viewers to followers.

- **Pro tip:** Mix broad (high-volume) and narrow (niche-specific) hashtags. Broad hashtags bring reach; niche tags bring relevance and higher conversion.

- **Bonus Pro tip:** I like to play a game with this. On any given hashtag, TikTok shows you the top 9 videos. I try to take as many of those top videos as possible, and I call it "Hijacked

Hashtag."

3) Trending-Audio Strategy Use trending audio intelligently, not blindly.

- **How:** Use trending songs/sounds as background, but adapt your hook and visuals to the vibe of the sound. The audio should *amplify* the message, not distract from it. Some trending sounds and songs can also have specific actions or trend elements that you should follow to maximize the effectiveness of using a trending song.

- **Why it works:** Trending audio gets a distribution boost; pairing it with a strong, bespoke hook doubles the chance it lands.

- **Tactics:**

  - **Sound + Hook Match:** If the sound is dramatic, match with suspenseful hooks. If it's upbeat, use quick onboarding lines and list formats.

  - **Micro-edits:** Sync cuts, text pops, and motion to the beat for higher retention.

  - **Rotate sounds:** If a hook works, test it over 3-5 trending sounds to see which yields higher watch time.

- **Pro tip:** If a sound is about to trend (you can often spot it on creator feeds), publish quickly; early adopters get the biggest boost.

4) Stitches & Duets Exploit social proof and existing virality.

- **How:** Stitch or Duet with trending, high-engagement videos in your niche, but always add clear value (explain, correct, extend, or demo).

- **Why it works:** You get exposed to the original video's audience and ride its existing momentum.

- **Pro tip:** When duetting, keep your on-camera reaction short and the added value long enough to justify rewatching.

5) Caption + First-Frame Hook Combo Thumbnail-like first 2 seconds + laser caption = scroll-stopper.

- **How:** Put your strongest hook visually in the first frame (text overlay). In the caption, use a single-line curiosity prompt (e.g., "Wait for #5..." or "Comment 'SHOW' for the guide").

- **Why it works:** Your first frame acts as a thumbnail in feeds; the caption gives the micro-CTA to drive comments.

- **Pro tip:** Keep overlay text to 3-6 words for instant readability.

6) Timing, Frequency & Analytics Tactics with rhythm and feedback.

- **Timing:** I'm probably the opposite of what most blogs or social media coaches will tell you. I typically don't care what time a video is posted. I think that's a crutch and a procrastination tactic. With that said, post during hours your audience is most active, use common sense, and test and check analytics to confirm.

- **Frequency:** Test volume, 1-3 daily, is common; if testing hooks, batch them to avoid audience fatigue.

- **Analytics loop:** Track watch time, completion rate, re-watch percentage, and comment growth. Let those metrics pick winners; scale winners quickly.

8) Safety & Authenticity Guardrails Always protect your account and your reputation.

- **Don't spam:** Targeted, value-first hijacking beats scatter-shot mass replies.

- **Don't mislead:** Ethical clickbait = intrigue that delivers. Avoid outright false claims.

- **Disclose when needed:** If you're promoting an affiliate or product, if your video is fully AI-generated, follow platform and legal disclosure rules.

- **Avoid harassment:** Don't feed or provoke toxic debates just for engagement. It damages brand equity. (I'm sure you've seen me do this. I speak from experience).

Execution Checklist (Quick Start)

- Pick one trending audio and 3 hooks for the same core video.

- Post the 3 tests back-to-back on TikTok.

- Identify 3 top creators in your niche for one daily Comment Hijack.

- Find 2 under-served hashtags and post 3 videos into them over the week.

- Track view rate, watch time, and new followers; scale winners.

TikTok Features to Master

1) Duets and Stitches: The Built-In Collaboration Engine

- **Duets** put your video side-by-side or top-bottom with someone else's. You can react, agree, disagree, or add context.

- **Stitches** let you take up to 5 seconds of another video and then add your own spin.

- **Why it works:** You're inserting yourself into conversations already getting attention. You're essentially using a proven winning video as your opening hook. (Quick plug, I actually indexed over 100 opening hooks you can download for free, that you can use as duets, at openinghooks .com). The original creator's audience sees your content, and you ride the wave of their virality.

- **Pro tip:** Always add value. Don't just nod or laugh; expand the idea, give a contrarian perspective, or show a better way to do it. That's what gets people to follow you, not just watch once. I think we've all seen those videos where someone just nods in the corner and they have added no value whatsoever! That's lazy content!

2) Green Screen and Filters

- TikTok rewards creators who use its native tools. Green screen, trending filters, and effects aren't just fun. They're discoverable features. These filters are actually clickable on your video and indexed into a feed of other videos using those filters.

- **How to leverage:**

  - Use the green screen feature to overlay yourself on top of screenshots, websites, videos, or tweets (X's?) you're talking about.

  - Jump on trending filters quickly. Every filter has its own discovery feed, meaning you're doubling your chances of being found.

- **Pro tip:** Pair a trending filter with a proven hook ("These 3 websites feel illegal to know") and you get both algorithm boosts at once, trending effect + engaging idea.

3) CapCut Templates

- TikTok owns CapCut. That means they prioritize content created with CapCut templates in the feed. Just like filters, CapCut templates are clickable on the video. When you click on it, it loads that template directly into your CapCut app on your phone.

- **Why it matters:** When you use a trending CapCut template, your video gets indexed not only in TikTok's main algorithm but also in the template's own search feed.

- **Execution:**

  - Open CapCut, browse trending templates.

  - Pick one that fits your niche: quote cards, "before/after" formats, list templates.

  - Drop in your own clips or screenshots, export, and publish straight to TikTok.

- **Pro tip:** Stay consistent. Even one CapCut template video per week can compound into thousands of additional views you wouldn't have gotten otherwise.

These three features, Duets/Stitches, Green Screen/Filters, and CapCut Templates, aren't gimmicks. They're distribution hacks. Each one is a backdoor into new discovery paths inside TikTok's algorithm. The more of them you stack into your posting routine, the faster you'll grow. You'll seem like you're a part of the conversation, and frankly, they're just a lot of fun.

TikTok is a Search Engine

Most people think TikTok is just an entertainment app. Wrong. TikTok is a search engine, and one of the most powerful in the world right now. Millions of people are literally typing their questions into TikTok's search bar instead of Google. If you're not creating content to answer those questions, you're invisible where your audience is actually looking.

Here's how to play the game:

1) Do Keyword Research Like a Pro

- Use free tools like **AnswerSocrates.com, AnswerTh ePublic.com**, or premium ones like **SEMrush.com** or Ahrefs.com. (Or... you could use my tool www.syllaby. io, which lets you do keyword research, optimizes your videos, and you can schedule and publish directly to Tik-Tok).

- Type in your niche keywords ("fitness," "estate planning," "AI tools").

- Export the list of *questions people are asking right now.*

2) Turn Questions Into Hooks

- Don't reinvent the wheel, just use their exact words.

- Example: "What's the best workout for beginners?" becomes your hook.

- Say it directly in the first 2 seconds of your video. TikTok hears it (yes, the algorithm listens), indexes it, and surfaces it when someone searches that question.

3) Deliver Expert Answers

- Keep it clear, simple, and valuable.

- Give your best advice in under 60 seconds.

- Always end with a **call to action** ("Follow for more AI tools" or "Comment GUIDE if you want the full checklist").

4) Proof That This Works I've helped "boring" industries, addiction treatment centers, law firms, and medical practices generate *hundreds of millions of views* using this exact strategy. Why? Because people are searching for those answers every single day.

Treat TikTok like YouTube in fast-forward: short, searchable, and packed with value. Do this consistently, and you'll own your niche on the platform.

Creator Search Insights

If you only take one thing from this chapter, let it be this: **TikTok is literally telling you what to post.**

Here's how:

1. **Open TikTok Search** Type in **"Creator Search Insights."** This is a feature most creators don't even know exists.

2. **What You'll Find**

   - **Trending Topics**: the exact subjects TikTok is surfacing as hot right now.

   - **Content Gaps**: areas where demand is high but supply

is low (translation: gold mines).

- **Audience Interest**: what people in *your* niche are searching for most.

- **Follower Search Queries**: what your own audience is actively typing into TikTok.

3. **Why This Matters** This is like having a cheat sheet from the algorithm itself. Instead of guessing or blindly following trends, you get a direct line to what people want to see.

4. **What to Do Next**

- Make a list of 10 topics from Creator Search Insights.

- Turn each into a question-style hook ("How to use ChatGPT?").

- Film those videos *this week*.

Don't overthink this. TikTok has already done the research for you. All you need to do is show up and answer the question with your own expertise.

Live Streaming Strategy

If you're not going Live on TikTok, you're leaving both reach and money on the table.

Here's the play:

- **Frequency:** Go live at least **once a week** for a **minimum**

of one hour. Short streams don't cut it. The algorithm rewards consistency and longer sessions. It takes time for TikTok's algorithm to actually push your feed out. So you'll notice that after you are live for a long time, you'll see a spike in viewership.

- **Discovery Power:** TikTok doesn't just show your live to followers. It actively pushes live streams to *new audiences*. That means every session is a chance to attract fresh people who've never seen your content before.

- **Growth Shortcut:** Some creators barely post regular content. They *only* livestream. And they still build massive, loyal audiences because of TikTok's distribution.

- **Direct Monetization:** Lives can pay you immediately. Viewers can send donations in the form of coins, Galaxies, and other gifts that convert directly into real money. You can also tap into the TikTok shop and sell things live. Combine this with community building, and you've got both reach and revenue.

Pro Tip: Treat your Live like a show. Plan themes, answer audience questions, share behind-the-scenes, or demo tools/products. To get the conversation rolling, ask small-talk questions like, "Where is everyone tuning in from?" or "What's something interesting that's happened to you recently?" You can also ask them to double-tap the screen to get likes for your live stream, which signals engagement. The more interactive you are, the more TikTok boosts your stream.

TikTok Shop

If you sell physical products or you're interested in affiliate marketing, **TikTok Shop is a no-brainer.** It lets you sell directly inside the app, turning TikTok from a discovery platform into a complete sales engine.

Here's why it's a game-changer:

- **Built-In Affiliate Network**: Other creators can promote your products for referral commissions. That means you don't have to rely only on your own reach; hundreds of micro-influencers can push your product for you.

- **Frictionless Checkout**: Customers never leave TikTok. They see your content, click, and buy, all without leaving the app. I personally have purchased many things through the TikTok shop, and the entire process from the moment you order to the time it arrives at your door is seamless. They notify you every step of the way. It's really amazing!

- **Live Stream Sales**: You can link products during your live streams and sell in real time while engaging with your audience. Think QVC meets TikTok.

- **A simple way to make money:** So if you're a content creator and you don't have anything physical to sell, you can easily sell other people's products on the TikTok shop. In fact, if you go to some products, you can even request a free sample be shipped to you in exchange for a video. When you create a video reviewing that product, you can link that video directly to the product, which is clickable on your video, and any time someone sees your video, clicks that link, and purchases the product, you get paid! This is affiliate marketing, and it's one of the easiest ways for new creators on TikTok to make money online.

- **Proven Results**: E-commerce brands are pulling in millions using TikTok Shop. The combination of algorithmic reach + built-in checkout is unlike anything else in social media right now.

Action Step for e-commerce sellers: If you sell a physical product, get your catalog into TikTok Shop immediately. Then start creating content (and partnering with creators) to drive sales.

Action Step for Content creators: Scroll through the TikTok shop and find products that your audience would be interested in, try to request a free sample if that product lets you, and start creating 3-5 videos for each product. Quick note: I've gotten everything from neck massagers, foot massagers, food, and even mushroom coffee for free in exchange for doing videos for the product on TikTok.

Your Bio Optimization

Your **username, name, and bio are prime real estate.** They're not just for branding, they're for discoverability.

- **Name:** This is separate from your username. This is what's displayed at the top of your profile. Most people just copy and paste their username in the Name field as well. But that is a wasted opportunity. This is actually indexable in search results. I have used this hack to find specific keywords on TikTok, personally and for clients. For example, I have a therapist client, and what we put in his name field was "Best Therapist in Orange County, CA."

- **Username:** This is your @handle that's branded. This is what you should probably keep universal across all of your social media accounts to be exactly the same.

- **Bio:** Think of your bio as a one-sentence elevator pitch. It should say who you help, what you do, and how people can get more from you. Example:

"Austin Armstrong, CEO of Syllaby.io

Preorder my first book: Virality!

Grow on Social Media and get paid with AI / ↓ "

- **Link:** Use the link in your bio strategically, whether it's your website, email list signup, or a LinkTree with affiliate products. Every viewer who clicks is a warm lead.

Your TikTok Action Plan

Week 1: Foundation

- Optimize your profile with a keyword-rich bio and name

- Research 20 trending hashtags in your niche

- Create your first 10 videos using different hooks

- Start following and engaging with 20 creators in your space

Week 2: Testing and Optimization

- Test 3 different hooks for the same piece of content

- Experiment with trending audio and effects

- Create video responses to comments on your content

- Track which video styles get the most engagement (we are looking for your series that you can repeat).

Week 3: Advanced Strategies

- Use **Creator Search Insights** to identify trending topics and content gaps

- Go live at least once a week

- Experiment with **Duets** and **Stitches** to jump into conversations

- Begin the **Hashtag Hijacking Strategy** for underserved keywords

Week 4: Scale and Systematize

- Implement the **75-15-5-5 funnel strategy** for content mix

- Repost your best-performing videos from the past 30 days

- If you have physical products, set up **TikTok Shop**

- Plan your next month of content using performance insights

The Truth About TikTok Timing

Stop obsessing over "optimal posting times." That advice is outdated and mostly useless. TikTok's algorithm doesn't care if you post at 7am or 11pm. It cares if your content holds attention and sparks engagement.

Great content always finds its audience. The algorithm distributes videos to small batches of users, measures performance, and then expands reach if the data looks good. Timing isn't the variable... quality is.

Your energy is better spent creating at scale, testing different hooks, and studying your analytics. **Consistency and quality will beat timing every single day.**

The Bottom Line

TikTok isn't just another social media app! It's your **testing ground, search engine, and money-printing machine** all rolled into one. While others get stuck worrying about dances, trends, or whether they're "too old" for the platform, you're going to use it strategically to build a content empire.

The timing could not be better with a US TikTok deal about to close. There's going to be a massive new wave of adoption of

TikTok, likely more than the original boom in 2020, especially for business owners.

TikTok rewards **experimentation, authenticity, and value.** It doesn't punish you for testing or failing; in fact, it gives you free market research and global distribution every single day.

You don't need youth. You don't need choreography. What you need is **value-driven content** delivered strategically to the right audience.

The opportunity is massive: over **1.6 billion active users worldwide** are searching for solutions to their problems right now. The only question is, are you going to be the one providing those solutions, or are you going to keep making excuses about why TikTok "isn't for you"?

Stop overthinking. Start creating. TikTok is waiting for you to step up.

Pick up your phone, press record, and start building your empire today.

What were your 3 key takeaways:

_____

_____

_____

What 3 additional action steps are you going to take:

_____

_____

_____

What is the deadline you're setting for each of these steps:

_____

_____

_____

Chapter 17: YouTube

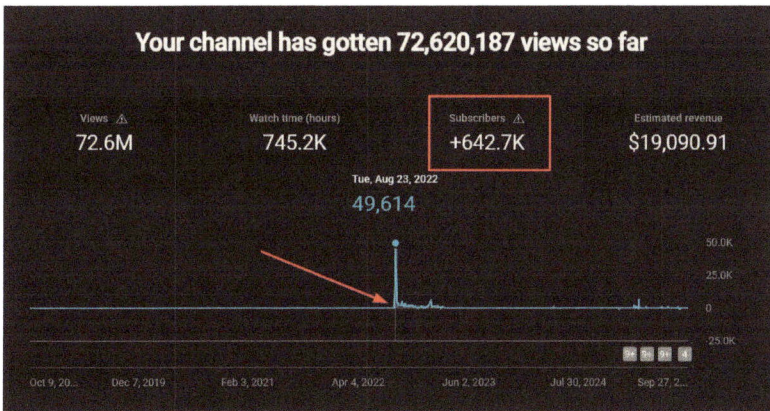

YouTube isn't just another social media platform; it's the world's second-largest search engine. If you're not treating it like that, you're playing the wrong game entirely.

For years, I didn't get it. I grinded. I posted over 600 videos. I spent three years testing, tweaking, and praying for traction. And what did I get? Barely 5,000 subscribers. Honestly, I was ready to quit.

TikTok was exploding. Instagram was sending me leads. Facebook has always generated quality leads. But YouTube? YouTube felt like trying to solve a puzzle with half the pieces missing.

Then everything changed in three days.

Not three months. Not three years. Three days.

I went from 5,000 subscribers to over 100,000. And it happened while I was sitting on a beach in Tulum, Mexico, watching my phone light up with notifications like a slot machine hitting the jackpot.

But this wasn't luck. This wasn't some random viral fluke. This was strategy. And in this chapter, I'm giving you the exact blueprint that cracked the code for me.

The Mentor Who Changed Everything

Jeremy Vest doesn't mess around. This is the guy who's helped brands like VidIQ, Braille Skateboarding, and Zapier rack up millions of subscribers and billions of views. So when he told me, *"Let's figure this out together,"* I knew I was about to get schooled.

For weeks, we jumped on daily Zoom calls. We dissected the DNA of viral channels like surgeons. We studied how top creators structured their videos, titled their Shorts for maximum curiosity, stacked hooks, and paced their scenes.

But here's the wild part, the game-changer wasn't some complicated editing trick or algorithm hack. It was something stupidly simple.

Upload strategy.

Until that point, I was doing what most creators do: shotgun posting. Every TikTok I made automatically went to YouTube. No filtering. No prioritizing. Just throwing everything at the wall and hoping something stuck.

Jeremy's advice was brutally simple: *Stop. Only post your best performers.*

The Strategy That Built My Empire

I had a TikTok series called *"These 5 Websites Feel Illegal to Know."* It had already racked up tens of millions of views. The format was curiosity-driven, top of funnel, practical, and insanely shareable.

So I tried something that felt almost too easy to work.

For one week, I posted nothing but those videos to YouTube Shorts, two to three per day. Same titles (Top 5 Most Useful Websites). Same content. Just my proven winners.

The algorithm grabbed them and ran.

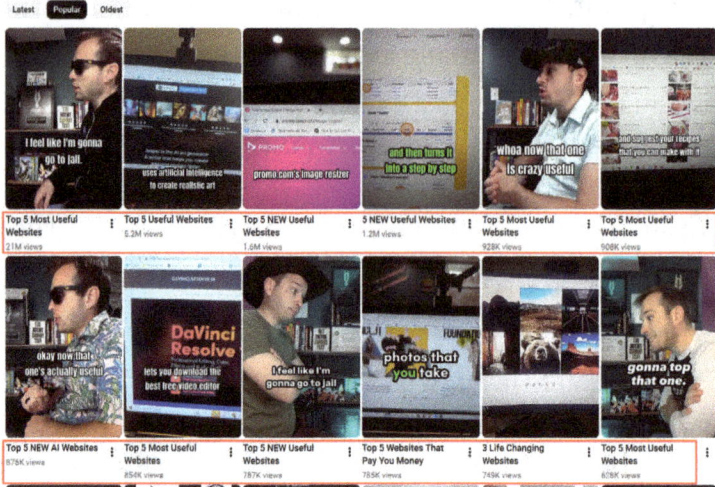

Here's what most people don't understand about YouTube Shorts: it's not about perfection. It's about proof. The platform rewards content that's already demonstrated it can hold attention and spark engagement.

Your upload strategy should be painfully simple:

- Only post content that's already proven successful on other platforms

- Focus on series and repeatable patterns, not random one-offs

- Upload 2–3 times per day when you find a winning format

- Then get out of the way and let the algorithm do the heavy lifting

This wasn't luck. It was strategy. And it's the same blueprint you can use to go from invisible to unstoppable.

The Title Formula That Never Fails

After studying my 600 failures, one truth became crystal clear: if I gave the information away in the title, performance tanked. But when I created intrigue, views skyrocketed.

Example:

- *Winning:* "Top 5 Most Useful Websites"

- *Losing:* "Top 5 Useful Websites for business owners and entrepreneurs"

The first is broad and curiosity-driven. It invites everyone in. The second is specific and limiting. It tells too much and narrows the audience.

Your sweet spot: broad enough to hook anyone, specific enough to deliver value.

Winning title patterns you can copy today:

- *"These X Things Feel Illegal to Know"*

- *"Here's What No One Tells You About X"*

- *"X Websites That Will Change Your Life"*

- *"Most People Are Doing X Wrong"*

And here's the part that will shock you: you can **reuse winning titles.** I've used *"Real Facts Confirmed in the Bible"* over 40 times on my Ancient History Facts channel. Most of them outperformed my "new" ideas.

Why? Because the algorithm doesn't care about originality. It cares about engagement. If a title format consistently pulls viewers in, keep using it until it stops working.

YouTube Thumbnails: Your Billboards To Views

Your thumbnail isn't just a preview image. It's a **billboard fighting for eyeballs** in a sea of endless content. And most creators? They half-ass it.

I'm not going to pretend I'm the world's leading thumbnail expert. There are incredible creators who specialize in this. But after studying them for over a decade, testing thousands of thumbnails across different industries, and watching the data pour in, I can tell you one thing for sure: **your thumbnail can make or break your video.**

High Contrast Wins Every Time

Your thumbnail needs to **pop off the screen.** Bold colors. Sharp text. Clear faces. If it doesn't stand out when shrunk to a postage stamp on a phone screen, it's useless.

Before you publish, search your topic on YouTube and study what's already ranking. What patterns do you see? Are they all similar? Great, then find one thing you can do differently to **stand out, not blend in.**

Text Should Tell a Story, Not Repeat Your Title

Don't just slap your video title on the thumbnail. Use the text to create **intrigue** or **emotion.** Instead of "5 AI Tools," try "GAME CHANGER" or "This Blew My Mind." Your **title and thumbnail should complement each other**, not compete for the same message.

Faces Beat Everything Else

Human psychology is simple: we're drawn to faces. If you're comfortable being on camera, put your face in the thumbnail, **and make it expressive.** Shocked. Excited. Confused. Whatever fits the story. People connect with people, not stock photos or logos.

The A/B Testing Game Changer

YouTube's new thumbnail A/B testing feature is an **absolute game-changer.** You can now upload multiple thumbnail options and let YouTube test them automatically to see which one gets the most clicks.

Most creators guess what works. Now you can know. Upload three variations, one with your face, one without, one brighter or darker, and let the data speak. Don't just test randomly. Test with intention. Each experiment should teach you something about what your audience responds to.

Stop Overthinking. Start Testing.

Creators waste hours perfecting one thumbnail. That's backwards. Create three **good** thumbnails instead of one "perfect" one, and let the algorithm decide.

Remember: **your thumbnail isn't art, it's marketing.** And in marketing, data always beats opinions.

Your job isn't to make the thumbnail you *like.* It's to make the thumbnail that gets *clicked.*

YouTube just handed you the tool to figure that out. **Use it.**

The Technical Details That Matter

Most creators overcomplicate YouTube. The truth? The technical side is simple if you know what actually moves the needle.

For Shorts:

- Keep videos **under 60 seconds**, even though YouTube currently supports up to 3 minutes.

- **Skip the tags.** They don't influence Shorts distribution.

- Descriptions don't matter. In fact, they completely removed clickable links on shorts descriptions.

- **No thumbnails needed.** Shorts don't use them in discovery. In fact, the only thing you can do is when uploading on the YouTube app on your phone, you can only select a single frame.

Pro Tip: In my experience, having uploaded and tested 1000s of YouTube shorts, the only things that seem to matter are the title and the view duration.

Pro Tip 2: If you have a long video that's related to a short, in the short, you can select a related video, which is a feature that directly connects to the long-form video. You can do this on the YouTube app or on the desktop.

For Long-Form Videos:

- Add a **pattern interrupt every 8-15 seconds** (cuts, zooms, text overlays, visuals, questions). This keeps attention locked.

- Use this structure: **Start with an opening hook —> Talk about a problem —> Align with the view to create credibility —> Resolve the problem with value —> Targeted call to action (tell them what to do next).**

- **Open loops in your intro.** Tease something you'll reveal later to keep viewers watching.

- Weave in **storytelling as a strategy.** Facts educate. Stories make people remember and share.

- Add easter eggs in each of your videos to create insider language. (See Chapter 12: Engagement Hacks)

Keep it simple. Nail these details and you'll outperform 90% of creators drowning in overthinking.

The YouTube Shorts Structure That Converts

Every successful YouTube short follows one simple pattern: **Hook —> Value —> Loop.**

- **Hook (first 3 seconds):** Stop the scroll instantly with a bold statement, question, or surprising fact. Example: *"These websites feel illegal to know."*

- **Value:** Deliver one clear tip, insight, or tutorial step. Keep it concise and useful.

- **Loop:** Re-engage your viewer with a twist or callback. Example: *"But here's what most people miss..."* This creates curiosity and makes people rewatch to catch the details.

Why it works: rewatches are algorithmic gold. When YouTube sees people watching your content again, it signals that your video is highly valuable, and the platform pushes it harder.

The Faceless Video Revolution

Not everyone wants to be on camera, and that's okay. In fact, some of my biggest YouTube wins came from **faceless channels**. One of them racked up **over a million views and 11,000 subscribers in just a few months** without me ever showing my face.

Here's the exact playbook:

1. Research and Recreation

- Study the top-performing videos in your niche.

- Break down their titles, hooks, and structure.

- Recreate the format with your own spin and insights.

- When something outperforms, turn it into a series. Audiences love consistency.

2. The Power of AI This is why I created my start-up, Syllaby, to allow people who cannot or will not be on camera to still get their ideas out there into the world with social media. Tools like **Syllaby.io** make this ridiculously easy. You can:

- Research trending topics across platforms

- Generate ready-to-go scripts

- Produce videos with AI voices, subtitles, and background music

- Schedule and publish across multiple platforms

It's not an exaggeration: you can automate an entire month of content in **minutes** using .

3. Call-to-Action Strategy Skip the generic "like and subscribe." Instead, use **identity-driven CTAs**:

- *"Subscribe if you love the Bible."*

- *"Follow if you're obsessed with AI tools."*

These connect to belonging, not obligation, and belonging is what actually drives people to hit that button.

The Volume Game Truth

YouTube success is a **volume game**, but not the way most people assume. It's not about cranking out random videos. It's about **testing variables** until you find what works, then doubling down relentlessly.

When you discover a winning format, whether it's a "Top 5 Websites" series or a specific tutorial style, **milk it dry.** Don't let boredom trick you into abandoning what's working. That's leaving money (and subscribers) on the table.

The algorithm loves consistency and patterns. If viewers keep showing up for the same type of content, YouTube connects the dots and pushes it to even more people. Your job is simple: figure out what the algorithm wants from your channel, and keep feeding it.

The Cross-Platform Multiplication Effect

YouTube doesn't exist in a vacuum. Your best-performing YouTube content is fuel for every other platform. The same broad, curiosity-driven titles that crush on YouTube also perform on Instagram Reels, TikTok, and even Facebook.

The rule is simple: **create once, distribute everywhere.** Start with what's already working, your proven winners. If a Short hits 1M views on YouTube, push it to TikTok, Instagram, Threads, Facebook, and LinkedIn.

Why reinvent the wheel when you can multiply the reach of content that's already proven to engage?

The Long-Game Reality

Here's what most YouTube gurus won't tell you: this game takes time. My breakthrough came after three years of grinding, three years of trial and error, failed experiments, and small wins that felt insignificant in the moment but were actually laying the foundation.

But here's what they also don't tell you: once it clicks, it compounds fast. What happened was when my one video went viral on YouTube, it seemed to have unlocked my entire channel. Every other video that was related to useful websites also started to blow up organically. It only took that one video to change the entire history of the channel.

Those three explosive days in Tulum weren't just about subscriber numbers shooting up. They were about freedom, the freedom to sit on a beach with someone you love, watching your phone light up like a jackpot machine, and knowing you've finally built something that works without you.

That's the real prize. Not just views. Not just money. Freedom.

Your Next Steps

Stop overthinking. Stop waiting for the "perfect" video. Stop treating YouTube like it's some mysterious, different beast.

Here's what to do:

1. Pick your two best-performing videos from any platform.

2. Post them to YouTube today.

3. Use a broad, curiosity-driven title.

4. Keep your description simple, title + call-to-action.

Then repeat tomorrow. And the next day.

The algorithm is waiting. Your audience is searching. Your competition is still hesitating.

The only thing standing between you and YouTube growth is action. Cut through the noise. Start today.

What were your 3 key takeaways:

_____

_____

_____

What 3 additional action steps are you going to take:

_____

_____

_____

What is the deadline you're setting for each of these steps:

_____

_____

_____

Chapter 18: LinkedIn

LinkedIn is the sleeping giant of social media, and most creators are sleeping on it.

For years, I've watched entrepreneurs, marketers, and creators overlook LinkedIn while chasing the latest flashy platforms. Big mistake. LinkedIn might be the single most profitable platform for business owners right now.

Here's the difference: while everyone else fights for scraps on TikTok, Instagram, and Facebook, LinkedIn is wide open. It's a slower burn, yes, but the creators who figure it out are stacking high-quality leads daily.

And the kicker? The same strategies that go viral on other platforms also work here. The difference is that LinkedIn's audience isn't just looking to be entertained. They have budgets, authority, and decision-making power.

Why LinkedIn Actually Works

I've tested my **hook —> problem —> solution —> call to action** format across every major platform. Guess what? It *crushes* on LinkedIn.

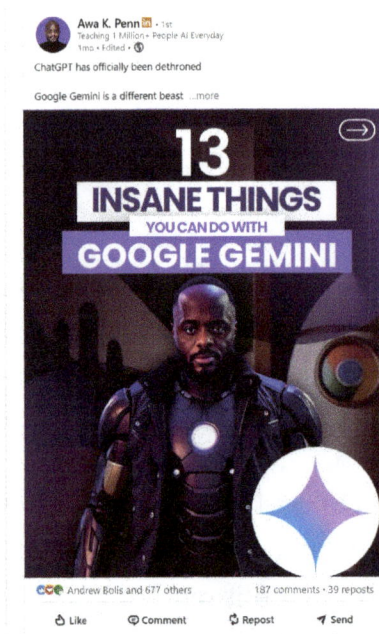

Take my friend **Awa K. Penn**. He's grown to 50,000 LinkedIn followers using the exact same strategies he uses on Facebook and Instagram. His posts consistently rack up hundreds of likes and comments because he sticks to the formula.

Here's one of his recent high-performers:

ChatGPT has officially been dethroned. Google Gemini is a different beast. I just compiled the best things you can now do with it:

—> Create Gems

—> Deep research

—> Kids storybooks

—> Guided learning

—> Convert audio to text

—> Convert videos to text

—> Create realistic images

—> Works across Google apps

—> Generate videos with Veo 3

—> Create quizzes on any topic

—> Create infographics in Canva

—> Build and edit web apps in Canvas

—> Create podcasts with Audio Overview

If you want more tips and insights about AI, join my newsletter that teaches you how to leverage AI.

The results? **676 likes, 186 comments, 37 reposts**.

Same structure. Same strategy. Different platform. And because LinkedIn users have decision-making power and budgets, this type of content translates into direct leads, sales, and brand deals, something most creators miss while chasing vanity metrics elsewhere.

The Content That Works

The posts that dominate LinkedIn aren't complicated. They're the same formula that works on Facebook, Instagram, and TikTok, because humans are humans everywhere.

Here's the exact structure:

1. Opening Hook: Grab attention immediately. Examples:

- *"Here's a list of six AI tools that can create presentations."*

- *"These 5 websites feel illegal to know."*

2. Problem: Call out the pain point.

- *"Presentations take hours to create."*

- *"Most people don't know how to use ChatGPT the right way."*

3. Solution: Deliver the quick win.

- *"Here's how you can create presentations in 30 seconds."*

- *"Here's the exact way to unlock ChatGPT's full power."*

4. Call to Action: Drive them where you want.

- *"Want my list of 150+ AI tools? Grab it here ."*

That's it. Simple. Repeatable. Scalable.

I've had LinkedIn posts reach **500,000+ views** using this exact framework. And yes, many of those links are affiliate offers, brand deals, or links to my own software companies. Just remember: you need to disclose them. The FTC requires it. Easy fix, put it in parentheses like *(affiliate link)* or make it clear in your call to action.

Building in Public Works Well on LinkedIn.

One of the biggest lessons I learned while building Syllaby: **don't build in stealth, build in public.**

Share your updates, lessons, and even failures openly. Start small, even if it's just one or two LinkedIn posts a week.

Why? Because people don't just follow products, they follow stories. They want to see the Hero's Journey. When your community feels like they have ownership in your journey, they cheer for your success.

LinkedIn is especially powerful for this strategy because its users *get* business challenges. They've been there. They've lived it. And they respect transparency.

Here's a story that shocked me: I was at NY Tech Week in New York City, and a guy walked up to me, nervous but excited. He told me he LOVES my LinkedIn content. That he'd been following me for years and learning from what I shared.

Now, I've been recognized before for my content, but never from LinkedIn. That one stopped me in my tracks. We shook hands, had a great 15-minute conversation about his professional journey, and it drove home a truth I'll never forget:

You never know who's watching. The lurkers, the quiet ones who never comment or like, are often your biggest fans. They're learning, absorbing, and one day they'll show up with an opportunity that changes everything.

What I Actually Do on LinkedIn

- **Same Framework, Different Lens:** I use the same **hook —> problem —> solution —> call to action** format that crushes on Facebook, TikTok, and YouTube. The difference? On LinkedIn, I frame everything in a way that resonates with professionals, entrepreneurs, and decision-makers.

- **Business Content First:** I share practical tips, business insights, and useful resources. My "5 websites that feel illegal to know" posts rack up millions of views on TikTok and YouTube, and those exact same posts perform on LinkedIn because professionals love efficiency hacks.

- **Visual Content Matters Here Too:** I don't just drop walls of text. I add images, graphics, and carousel posts. Visuals cut through the scroll on LinkedIn just like they do everywhere else.

- **Value, Then Offers:** The same rule applies everywhere: give away your best information for free, then sell the implementation. When I provide clear, actionable value upfront, people trust me, and when I finally make an offer, they're ready to say yes.

LinkedIn Videos

LinkedIn has always been a little late to the game on new features, but when they do roll something out, they roll it out strong. Case in point: **vertical video.**

LinkedIn now has a dedicated **video feed** that feels almost identical to TikTok. When you scroll your homepage, you'll also notice "trend areas", curated topics where LinkedIn showcases trending video conversations. Examples I've seen include:

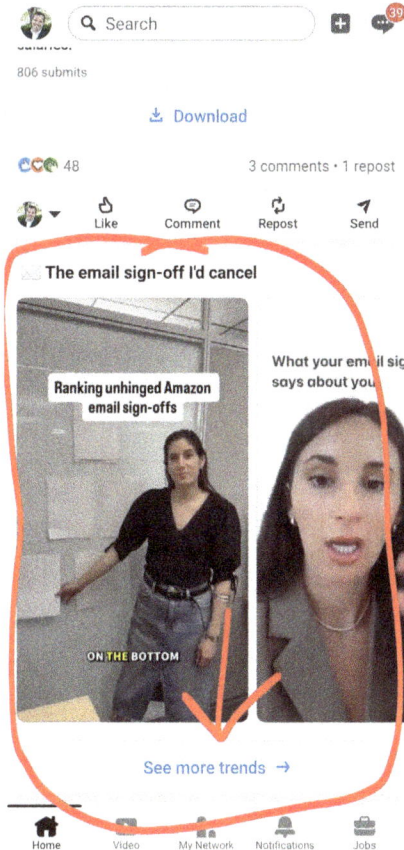

"The 5 to 9 before my 9 to 5" (highlighting morning routines)

"The email sign-off I'd cancel" (playful commentary on workplace culture)

You can swipe through these trending videos and join the conversation to boost discovery, or click **"See more trends"** to view the full list of top video series for the day.

This is LinkedIn's way of nudging you toward what's hot *right now*. If you jump in early, you can ride that wave of distribution while the feature is still fresh.

This is one of the most underrated ways to get found on LinkedIn and generate leads for your business. The supply-demand gap is massive: **very few people are creating video on LinkedIn, but almost everyone is consuming it.** That's your opportunity.

I recommend posting **2-3 videos per week**. That cadence is enough to stay visible without overwhelming yourself, and it's plenty to dominate in a space where competition is still low.

Pro Tip: When you post a video, don't just drop the video and go. Pair it with a long, text-based description, ideally close to the full transcript of your video. Why? Because many people scroll LinkedIn while they're at work. They can't always have the sound on, but they *can* read.

And don't forget **hardcoded subtitles** on the video itself. This removes every ounce of friction for your audience to consume your content however they prefer, silently or with audio.

The easier you make it for people to engage, the more leads you'll capture.

LinkedIn Newsletters

One of the most underutilized features on LinkedIn right now? **Newsletters.**

I'll give credit where it's due: my friend Judi Fox (my own LinkedIn coach) pushed me for years to use this feature before I finally listened. And she was right.

Here's why they're so powerful:

- **Built-In Subscribers**: Just like any email platform, you get subscribers, open rate data, and engagement metrics.

- **Multiple Newsletters**: You're not limited to one. You can run different newsletters for different audiences or niches.

- **SEO Goldmine**: This is the killer feature. LinkedIn has massive authority with Google. When you post a newsletter, you can optimize the **URL, SEO title, and meta description**. That means your newsletter can rank on Google and pull in free traffic.

If you already run an email newsletter, don't reinvent the wheel; just repurpose it here. Copy, paste, polish, publish. Instant extra reach.

Or, if you're starting fresh, create an industry-specific newsletter: share curated news, weekly tips, or interviews tailored to your target audience.

Post at least **once per week**. That cadence is enough to build momentum and stay top of mind with subscribers, while sending strong signals to both LinkedIn and Google.

The Truth About LinkedIn Growth

Here's the reality: **LinkedIn isn't mysterious, it's predictable.**
The platform rewards the same fundamentals every other social
network does:

- **Strong hooks** that stop the scroll

- **Content that solves real problems** (not fluff)

- **Clear calls to action** so people know the next step

- **Consistent posting** that builds trust

- **Genuine engagement** with your audience

Start Small, But Start

If you're not active on LinkedIn yet, here's my advice: **start small.**
Even one or two posts per week is enough to begin building
momentum.

Don't overthink it. Don't wait for the perfect content plan or the
flawless posting schedule. **Perfection is procrastination.**

You already have the blueprint. The same content frameworks,
the same engagement strategies, the same lead-generation tactics
from this book work here too.

The only thing standing between you and LinkedIn growth is
action.

So cut through the noise, post that first piece of content, and start today.

What were your 3 key takeaways:

_____

_____

_____

What 3 additional action steps are you going to take:

_____

_____

_____

What is the deadline you're setting for each of these steps:

_____

_____

_____

Chapter 19

Affiliate marketing

I said this at the very beginning of this book, and I want to say it again here to really drive it home: **shift your mindset.** Stop thinking of yourself as "just a content creator" and start thinking like a **business owner who creates content.**

Let's clear the air right now: **affiliate marketing is not a pyramid scheme, MLM hustle, or any other scammy nonsense.** I can't believe I even have to say that, but too many people confuse it with those shady models.

The reality: **Affiliate marketing is just commission-based sales.** Plain and simple.

Think about buying a car. You walk into a dealership, talk to a salesperson, and when you buy, that salesperson earns a commission. That's it. That's affiliate marketing, except instead of selling cars, you're promoting **software, tools, courses, or services online.**

But here's where it gets **beautiful**, and where most people completely miss the boat. Unlike car sales or Amazon affiliates, where you get a **one-time commission**, the real money is in **recurring revenue.**

When you promote **SaaS tools** (software-as-a-service), you don't just get paid once. You get paid **every single month** that the customer keeps their subscription; you get paid, typically, 20%–50% of their subscription fee. That means:

- Sell once.

- Get paid forever.

- Watch your commissions stack month after month like clockwork.

This is the shift that turns affiliate marketing from "extra cash" into a **life-changing income stream.** If you're relying solely on ad revenue, you're playing the wrong game.

I prefer a smarter model: **recurring commissions.**

One-Time Commission vs. Recurring Commission

To put this into perspective, I currently promote around 60 different AI and software tools. Some generate small payouts, while others have completely changed my financial reality. One tool in particular, has consistently earned me between **$15,000 and $20,000 a month in recurring commissions** for the past two years. Think about that: one tool, one relationship, one affiliate link. It didn't happen overnight, but with consistency, it turned into a steady five-figure monthly income stream.

So how do I drive these results? I use what I call a **multi-channel affiliate funnel.**

A quick disclaimer as well: You must disclose when a link you promote is an affiliate link. The FTC requires it. Be smart, and always disclose when you get a commission for promoting something. Plus, it builds trust and credibility with your audience. Most people want to find a way to support you anyway!

First, I make sure all of my affiliate links are easily accessible. I use a bio tool like LinkTree, Beacons, or Stan Store so I can feature multiple clickable links at once. That way, no matter what I'm promoting that week, my audience can find it instantly.

Second, my content engine runs on **short-form video and text threads.** I create Reels, TikToks, Shorts, Clips, and text threads, specifically on Facebook, that highlight the tools I'm affiliated with, and I post them everywhere, Instagram, YouTube, TikTok, Facebook, Threads, X, and even Pinterest. Every video follows the S.T.A.R.T. Framework you saw earlier in the book, which keeps them engaging and built to convert.

Third, I add **automation into the mix.** On Instagram, I'll say something like, *"Comment the word SYLLABY and I'll DM you the link!"* Then, tools like ManyChat or Go High Level take over. They instantly send the resource or affiliate link, and with Go High Level, I can even add that person to my CRM for future follow-ups via email or text. That one layer of automation has turned thousands of casual comments into long-term leads.

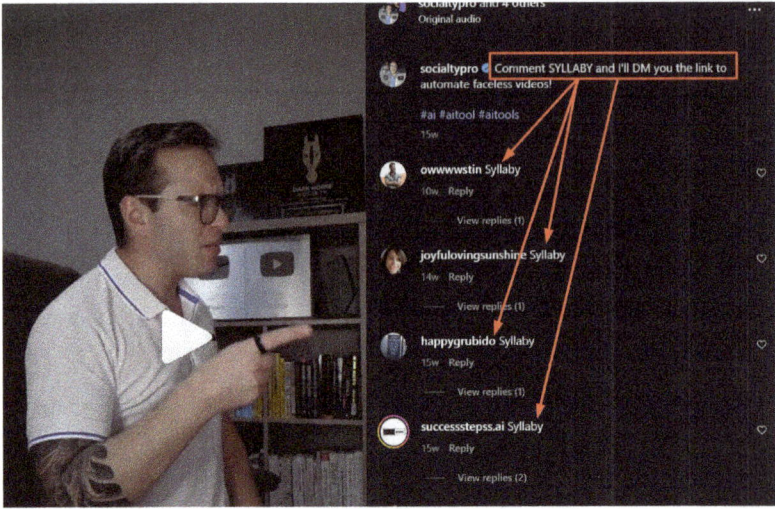

Fourth, I leverage **text-based threads** on platforms like Facebook, X, LinkedIn, and Threads. Right now, those platforms are giving massive organic reach to text posts. I'll start with a bold, curiosity-driven headline like: *"RIP SEO agencies! This one AI tool does everything they do, but 10X cheaper."* Then I'll post 3-5 comments underneath explaining exactly how the tool works, like how Ranked.ai writes and publishes blog articles, does backlink outreach, and tracks your SEO growth.

That newsletter has become the glue that holds everything to-gether. Every video, every thread, every collab leads people back to it. And it consistently grows by **100-200 new subscribers a day.** Inside the newsletter, I give even more tutorials and case studies, and of course, more affiliate recommendations. These multiple touch-points, video, automation, threads, and email, work together like a charm. People rarely buy the first time they see something. But after three, four, or five touch-points? That's when the conversions start stacking.

How to find affiliate programs you can promote

This is a great question that I get asked constantly. Most software tools will have some sort of affiliate or referral program. The tricky nuance is that they can be called different things, like Affiliate program, partner program, referral program, etc. And they can also be found in different locations on a company's website. Sometimes they're in the footer of the website, sometimes in the top navigation, and some you can't access unless you actually sign up first!

With that said, where I typically start is simply with the tools I use frequently. I've found that when I promote a software tool that I actually use, I can not only talk confidently about it, but I can also show my own outcomes and examples. This can help convert a lot more affiliate sales for you.

If you're not using that many software tools, you can search on directories like , , , , or for thousands of tools in any industry you can think of!

Lastly, for reference, these are my favorite affiliate programs that have worked out best for me personally.

1. www.Ranked.ai

2. www.Syllaby.io (I own this tool for reference)

3. www.GoHighLevel.com

4. www.Tella.TV

5. www.Repurpose.io

And that's the secret to affiliate marketing: it's not about one viral video or one affiliate link. It's about building a system that compounds. At first, you might make $50 here and $100 there. But if you keep posting, keep automating, keep building your list, and keep stacking recurring offers, those small wins snowball into something life-changing.

Affiliate marketing isn't a short-term "get rich quick" scheme. It's a long game. But if you commit, it's one of the most predictable, scalable, and sustainable income streams you can build as a content-driven entrepreneur.

If you'd like to see specific examples of how I'm doing this, my full list of 60+ tools I'm an affiliate for, and an affiliate marketing masterclass webinar, you can visit to find free affiliate marketing trainings and examples.

My Complete Affiliate Marketing System

Here's my exact process, step by step. I'm giving you everything because I want you to win

Step 1: The AI Content Creation Engine

I use ChatGPT to automatically generate daily affiliate content in the exact format that converts on Facebook.

How I set it up:

1. **Start a new ChatGPT chat** (on Plus or better).

2. **Use ChatGPT tasks** to produce content daily in a strict format.

   a. To use tasks and set up a recurring automation inside ChatGPT, start a new chat, and start your prompt with "every day at xyz time do this thing."

3. **Feed it 10-15 of your best-performing threads** as examples so it learns your voice, hooks, and CTA style.

4. **Lightly edit** the daily drafts (add your story, proof, numbers), then post.

The outcome: Every day, I get a fresh, on-brand thread like: *"Rest in peace, PowerPoint. These 5 AI tools create presentations in 30 seconds."* It includes a clean headline, 5 punchy bullets, and a CTA I can rotate (newsletter, YouTube, affiliate link). My Facebook profile is monetized, so I get paid on engagement, **and** I stack **recurring affiliate commissions** when people click through.

Cost: about **$20/month** for ChatGPT Plus. That's it.

Copy-and-Paste Prompt (use as your base)

Role & Style You are my content engine. Write Facebook text threads in my voice: practical, punchy, no fluff.

Format Rules

- No emojis, no em dashes.

- Max 2 lines in the **headline hook**.

- Then **5 short bullets** (1-2 lines each), each a standalone actionable tip.

- Finish with **one clear CTA** (newsletter, YouTube, or affiliate tool, rotate evenly).

- Reading level: simple, skimmable, high-contrast phrasing.

Topic Source Use the patterns from the examples below. Prioritize evergreen, broad-appeal topics that solve a tangible problem and spark curiosity.

Output Cadence Every day at 10:00 AM Eastern, generate **3 unique thread options** on [MY NICHE] so I can pick the best one.

Examples to Imitate (tone/structure) [PASTE 10–15 of your top-performing threads here]

Today's Topics to Propose

1. [Topic A] 2) [Topic B] 3) [Topic C]

Pro tips to dial it in:

- Add: "Hook must feel like a magazine cover. Avoid 'fluff' verbs (optimize, leverage), use concrete actions."

- Add: "Each bullet should stand alone (no numbering dependencies)."

- Add: "CTA variants: (1) 'DM **GROWTH** for the full checklist', (2) 'Grab the free SOP in my bio', (3) 'Watch the 5-min tutorial on YouTube (link in comments)'."

Posting workflow (60 seconds each)

1. **Main post (hook only):** Use a **colored background** (black/white pops).

2. **Comment stack:** Paste each bullet as a **separate comment** (1 per comment).

3. **Final comment = CTA:** newsletter / YouTube / affiliate link (rotate).

4. **Optional:** Share your post to **5-10 relevant groups** over 24-48 hours.

Guardrails that make this convert (and keep you safe)

- **Disclose** when a link is an affiliate (simple: "affiliate link").

- Use **UTM tags** on affiliate links so you can see which

platforms drive revenue.

- **Rotate CTAs** so you grow **multiple assets** (list, YouTube, offers), not just one.

- Keep a **"Winners" folder**: save threads that outperform; recycle them in 30-45 days.

- If a draft reads generic, prompt: "Make each bullet more specific; include a tool, step, or example."

Step 2: The Strategic Post Structure

Every post I create follows the exact same framework. Why? Because it works.

The Formula:

1. **Hook:** A bold headline that stops the scroll.

2. **Problem:** Talk about a specific problem that relates to the viewer based on the opening hook.

3. **Value:** 5 specific tools, tips, or strategies that solve a real problem.

4. **Call to Action:** A clear next step (affiliate link, email signup, or another platform).

The Format:

- On Facebook, I always use a **black background with white text**. It's high contrast, takes up more real estate, and instantly grabs attention in the feed.

- The **headline goes in the main post.**

- Each value point gets its own **separate comment.**

- The **final comment is always the CTA.**

Why this works: Since Facebook doesn't order comments chronologically, people scroll and hunt for the next step, artificially boosting engagement and reach.

Mini Checklist for Every Post

- Hook in the main post (black background, white text)

- Downward finger emojis () telling people to check comments

- Separate comments for each value point

- Final comment = CTA (affiliate link, email list, or other platform)

- Optional: share into 5-10 niche groups for more reach

Step 3: The Email List Funnel

Not every post should slam an affiliate link. In fact, many of my best-performing posts drive people into my **email newsletter** first.

Here's why that works:

- **Free Value First:** When someone signs up, they immediately get my "List of Useful AI Websites." It's a clean, organized resource that looks like a cheat sheet, *but it's actually built from my affiliate links.* They get value, I get recurring clicks. For ease of access, it's just simply a read-only Google Sheet organized by the name of the tool, the link to the tool, and a brief description of what it is and who it helps.

  - **Pro Tip:** Have a really strong CTA to sign up for your list. For example, the one I use is "Want my list of my top 150+ AI tools? Get it here for free: example.com"

- **Recurring Touch-points:** Once they're on my list, I can promote tools week after week without relying on the algorithm.

  - **Pro Tip:** This is my weekly email marketing cadence: Twice a week, I send a dedicated AI newsletter about all of the latest AI news to provide value. And three times a week, I send a dedicated email on one particular tool that I'm an affiliate for. It's a deep dive into how to use that tool and who or how it helps.

- **Monetized Growth:** I use **Beehiiv** for my newsletter. Their "Boost Program" actually **pays me for every new subscriber** I send, so my list literally grows while generating cash. Each new subscriber is offered the opportunity to subscribe to a set of other newsletters related to mine. If they do, I get paid for each email that signs up because those other newsletters are paying through Beehiiv to grow their list from other creators.

- **Weekly Conversions:** Every week, my newsletter (shoutout to Dawn and Rhea, who help me run it) includes "Top Tools of the Week." Readers see it as curated value, while I stack more affiliate clicks in the background.

This is the difference between **short-term commissions** and **long-term wealth.** Social platforms come and go, but once someone's on your email list, you own that relationship forever.

Step 4: The Facebook Group Strategy

Here's where most people blow it: they chase **short-term clicks** instead of **long-term relationships**.

I run a Facebook ecosystem that feeds itself: my posts reach **200-300M people/month** and I've got **2.1M+ followers**. When people engage with my public content, I've set up **auto-invites** so they're prompted to join the **Syllaby** Facebook group. That group is now **65,000+ members** strong, sharing wins and success stories daily. New people see that social proof and immediately ask, *"What is Syllaby?"* or *"Will this work for my niche?"*, which opens the door for helpful answers (and ethical monetization).

We have a game that we like to play in the group: "Beat Me to the Response."

Your job: **be first, be helpful, then softly recommend.** When a member asks a question, jump in fast with a clear, valuable mini-answer. Only **after** you've helped, add your affiliate link as the natural next step.

Value-First Reply Framework (VFRF)

1. **Acknowledge the goal**: "Great question, most [niche] run into this at step one."

2. **Give a 3-step micro-solution**: quick, doable, specific.

3. **Add one pro tip/tool** that removes friction.

4. **Soft CTA + disclosure**: "If you want my exact setup, here's the tool I use (affiliate link). Happy to share a mini SOP if you want it." (SOP = Standard Operating Procedures)

Copyable response template

You're on the right track. Here's a quick way to test this without wasting hours:

1. Do X to validate Y in 10 minutes.

2. Use the Z setting to avoid the common mistake.

3. Record the result and adjust once. *If you want my exact workflow, I use [Tool] (affiliate link) because it automates steps 2-3. If you'd like, I can drop a mini checklist here.*

Set Up Your Group Flywheel

- **Link your group to your business page or profile** (professional mode must be turned on) and turn on the auto-invite feature in your professional dashboard (so engagers see the invite).

- **Seed social proof**: pin member wins, before/afters, and FAQ answers so new folks see value instantly.

  - **Pro Tip:** We hold daily challenges in the group with themes like sharing your biggest takeaways, sharing your affiliate marketing wins, and your biggest Syllaby growth hacks.

- **Make it easy to help**: keep a running doc of your best answers so you can paste, personalize, and post fast.

Do's and Don'ts (so you don't get banned)

- **Do** read each group's rules; some require no links in top-level comments (drop the link in a follow-up comment).

- **Do** add a simple **disclosure** ("affiliate link") when you link.

- **Do** prioritize **teaching over pitching**; your help is your differentiation.

- **Don't** dump links without context. **Don't** argue with mods. **Don't** post the same reply verbatim everywhere.

E Mini Checklist (run this every time)

- Be the **first useful answer** (speed matters).

- Give **one quick win** they can do in <10 minutes.

- Offer the **tool/workflow** as an optional next step.

- Add **disclosure** if you link.

- Log the thread (question, date, link clicks via UTM, conversions) to see what's working.

Why this works: Groups are concentrated, problem-aware audiences. When you show up as the **most helpful person in the room**, you become the default recommendation. That earns trust, drives recurring traffic, and compounds your affiliate revenue, without ever feeling spammy.

Step 5: The Distribution Amplification

Create once, distribute everywhere. That's the mindset.

When I publish a thread or post on my Facebook page, I don't let it sit there waiting for the algorithm to do its thing. I take that same piece of content and **share it in 5-10 highly relevant Facebook groups**. Same effort to create, 10x the reach.

Here's how to make it work:

1. **Find the Right Groups:** Search for groups in your niche,

AI tools, business automation, marketing strategies, fitness, real estate, whatever fits your lane. Bigger is good, but engagement matters more than size. A 5K-member group with active discussions will outperform a 100K-member ghost town.

2. **Become a Known Name First:** Don't just join and dump links. Engage first. Comment on other posts. Answer questions. Add value without dropping a link. That way, when you finally share your own posts, you're seen as a contributor, not a spammer.

3. **Post Valuable Content (Not Ads):** Your posts should solve problems, teach something new, or save people time. The affiliate links are secondary. When people get value, they'll naturally click through to learn more.

4. **Play by the Rules:** Some groups don't allow links in posts, so adapt. Post the main content in the group, then say: *"I've put the full resource + tools in the comments (affiliate link)."*

Distribution Checklist

- Share each new post into 5-10 groups within 24 hours

  - **Pro Tip:** Try not to do more than this to avoid Facebook spam limitations.

- Lead with value (problem —> solution —> resource)

- Respect group rules & culture

- Rotate CTAs: affiliate link, newsletter, YouTube, etc.

Bottom line: Don't treat groups like dumping grounds. Treat them like mini-communities. If your content genuinely helps, group distribution will multiply your reach and your revenue.

The Global Opportunity

Here's one of the most beautiful things about affiliate marketing: **geography doesn't matter.**

Whether you're in Berlin, Bangladesh, Nigeria, or Kentucky, you get paid the same commissions I do. Affiliate programs don't care where you live.

For my friends in countries where Facebook monetization isn't available, this is your goldmine. You might not be able to earn directly from Facebook payouts, but you can absolutely build a recurring affiliate income stream. I personally know creators outside the U.S. stacking **$10K, $15K, even $20K per month**, just through affiliate commissions. That's not hype, that's reality.

And let's be real: $20,000 a month is life-changing money almost anywhere in the world.

But here's what you need to understand: **this isn't a get-rich-quick scheme.**

- You have to show up daily.

- You have to provide value consistently.

- You have to give it time, months, *sometimes years*, not weeks.

Most people quit. That's the brutal truth. They expect life-changing results in 30 days, don't see them, and walk away. But the people who stick with it for 6 months, 12 months, 3 years, those are the ones who build freedom businesses that pay them every single month, no matter where they live.

If you're outside of the U.S. and can't monetize directly through Facebook, don't see that as a disadvantage. See it as clarity: **affiliate marketing is your path to wealth.**

Advanced Automation Strategies

Ready to go beyond manual posting and really scale? This is where automation flips the game. With the right tools, you can turn your affiliate marketing into a **24/7 revenue machine** running across multiple platforms at once.

Here's how I do it with **Syllaby**:

1. **Create a Bulk Video Campaign** Pick a topic in your niche (AI, fitness, real estate, history, whatever lane you're in). In the bulk scheduling feature, you just enter in one topic and Syllaby will automatically create up to 150 unique topics, titles, and video scripts for you.

2. **Connect All Your Socials** Hook up TikTok, YouTube, Instagram, Facebook, Threads, and LinkedIn.

3. **Automate Posting** Set the system to push out **5 videos**

per day for 30 days straight. That's **150 pieces of content** auto-published across 6 platforms, 900 posts total.

4. **Affiliate CTA in Every Description** Every single video includes your affiliate link in the description or pinned comment. That's hundreds of touch-points working for you on autopilot.

5. **Track + Refine** Use analytics to double down on the hooks and formats that drive the most clicks.

Proof this works: I'm literally doing this right now with my **Ancient History Facts channel.** Fully automated, consistently growing, and quietly stacking affiliate commissions while I sleep.

Since you're here reading this book, let me break down why the **Syllaby affiliate program** is different, and why it's built for you to actually succeed.

Most affiliate programs hand you a link and basically say, *"Good luck."* We don't roll like that. With Syllaby ( ), you're set up with:

- **30% Lifetime Commissions** Not one-time, not capped, not expiring. If someone signs up through your link, you get paid **every single month** they stay a customer.

- **60-Day Cookie Window** Somebody clicks your link today and buys 2 months later? You still get full credit.

- **Complete Resource Library** Plug-and-play videos, scripts, email templates, banner images, and swipe files so you're never starting from scratch.

- **Active Community Support** Join a network of other affiliates who share strategies, wins, and insights. Collaboration > competition.

- **Real Training and Guidance** We don't just drop a link in your lap. We give you coaching and frameworks to build real recurring revenue.

With Syllaby, you're not just another affiliate; we see you as a partner. When you win, we win. That's why we've stacked the deck in your favor.

7 Day Affiliate Kickstart Plan

Day 1 - Pick Your Winning Tool

- Research 3–5 SaaS tools in your niche, by using resources like: producthunt.com, theresanaiforthat.com, fastpedia. io, or futuretools.io

- Choose **one** you actually use and believe in (authenticity matters).

- Sign up for its affiliate program and grab your unique link.

Day 2 - Set Up Your Affiliate Hub

- Create a **LinkTree-style page** (or use others like Stan Store, Beacons, or Go High Level).

- Add your affiliate link with a clear label (e.g., *"My #1 SEO Tool"* instead of a random URL).

- Keep your bio link clean and focused, with a call to action as the last line in the description. (ex: "grab my favorite AI tools here ")

Day 3 - Record Your First Short-Form Video

- Use the **S.T.A.R.T. framework** (from earlier in the book).

- Film a 30–60 second Reel/TikTok about the tool: hook —> problem —> value —> call-to-action.

- Example CTA: *"Comment SEO and I'll DM you the link to the exact tool I use."*

Day 4 - Automate Your Funnel

- Set up **ManyChat** or **Go High Level**.

- Program a trigger word (e.g., "SEO" or "STRATEGY") that auto-replies with your affiliate link + a bonus resource.

- Test it on yourself to make sure it works smoothly.

Day 5 - Repurpose Everywhere

- Take your Day 3 video and post it to TikTok, Instagram Reels, YouTube Shorts, Facebook Reels, Threads, X, and Pinterest.

- Remember: **1 video = 7 platforms = 7 audiences**.

Day 6 - Add Depth with a Text Thread

- Create a mini-thread on Threads, X, or Facebook, using a

tool like threadmaster.ai (that I created, by the way).

- Start with a bold headline (e.g., *"RIP SEO agencies. This AI tool does 10x the work for a fraction of the cost."*).

- Follow with 3-5 comments teaching something valuable. Drop your link in the final comment.

Day 7 - Build Your Email List

- Add a **newsletter opt-in** to your LinkTree page ("Get my free weekly growth tips").

- Start sending at least 1 email per week.

- Pro tip: Your first email can reintroduce the same affiliate tool with a short tutorial; repetition builds conversions.

- Bonus Pro tip: I recommend, and personally use, beehiiv .com as my email newsletter platform

At the end of 7 days, you'll have:

- A chosen affiliate offer

- A functioning bio hub

- Your first short-form video live on 7 platforms

- DM automation in place

- A text thread driving traffic

- An email list started

Basically, your **entire affiliate marketing machine** will be running in one week. But *you* need to act on this.

The Reality Check

Here's the part most people gloss over: **your first few months will probably suck.**

You'll post threads that flop. You'll see $2.17 in commissions and wonder if this was a waste of time. You'll question whether affiliate marketing *actually works.*

That's normal.

When I say I make $15,000-$25,000 a month from Ranked.ai, that's not overnight money. I've been promoting it consistently for **three years.** One post didn't do it. One month didn't do it. But showing up daily did.

The people earning serious affiliate income are the ones who **treat it like a business, not a hobby.** They don't post when inspiration strikes. They post every day. They don't drop links and ghost; they engage, answer questions, and provide value daily.

There are no shortcuts. But if you follow this system and commit to showing up consistently, you'll build something that compounds, generating **recurring revenue streams that pay you for years.**

That's location independence. That's financial freedom. That's the ability to help people discover tools that actually improve their lives, *and get paid for it.*

The opportunity is right in front of you. You now have the exact blueprint that generates me **five figures a month in recurring affiliate revenue.**

The only question is:

 Are you going to keep making excuses?

 Or are you going to get to work?

Stop making excuses. Start making money.

Now go execute.

What were your 3 key takeaways:

_____

_____

_____

What 3 additional action steps are you going to take:

_____

_____

_____

What is the deadline you're setting for each of these steps:

_____

_____

_____

Chapter 20

The Future Of What We Sell Online

A massive shift is happening right now, and I'm doing everything I can to lead it.

We're moving away from traditional info products like ebooks and online courses toward something I call **"vibe-coded Micro SaaS."**

Think about this concept: Ebooks, courses, and info products **teach** your clients what to do. But Micro SaaS **does it for them**, helping them increase their likelihood of getting results.

I've been saying this loudly in my talks and social posts:

"Ebooks are dead. Vibe-coded Micro SaaS is the new lead magnet and low-ticket offer."

If you're newer to the AI space, that might sound like sci-fi jargon. Stick with me, it's not. It's the next evolution of digital entrepreneurship.

Micro SaaS (Software as a Service) is simply a small, non-complex software tool that solves *one specific problem*.

I've launched several of these:

- **ThreadMaster.ai:** Creates viral text threads for Facebook, X, and LinkedIn.

- **ScriptStorm.ai:** Generates viral video scripts using my S.T.A.R.T. framework.

- **FastPhoto.io:** Creates professional AI headshots in seconds.

- **Bibley.io:** An AI-powered Bible study assistant.

Each one does exactly one thing, and that's the point. They're affordable ($4.99–$9.99/month), easy to market, and build predictable recurring revenue.

Vibe coding is software creation powered by plain English. You describe what you want an app to do, and an AI large-language model (LLM) writes the code for you, no developer experience needed.

If you've used ChatGPT, you can build software.

Platforms like **Lovable, Bolt, Manus, Replit, and Base44** are pioneering this space. You literally type:

"I want an app that creates daily affirmations, emails them to users, and has a dark-mode dashboard."

The AI designs it, codes it, hosts it, and helps you refine it, all through conversation.

While vibe coding isn't perfect yet (security and bug issues can still pop up), it's *shockingly fast.* My personal workflow: I vibe-code 90% of the app, then bring in a real developer to finalize and deploy it. The result? **Idea to live software in days.**

I'm currently building and launching a new Micro SaaS every 14 days, and selling them using the exact social media strategies in this book.

Ebooks, courses, and info products **teach** people what to do. But Micro SaaS **does it for them.**

Think about it. How many times have you bought a course or ebook and never finished it? We've all been there. With software, you're giving your audience a *shortcut to implementation.*

And here's the kicker: Courses and ebooks are one-time payments. Micro SaaS = recurring revenue.

That means your customer lifetime value skyrockets while your audience actually gets results.

Over the next few years, you're going to see a flood of simple, single-purpose tools hit the market. Most will be built with vibe coding.

The barrier to entry is gone. The cost is minimal. The potential is enormous.

This is your chance to stop just teaching and start **building.** To go from giving information to giving transformation. To move from "learning" to "doing."

Your audience doesn't just want knowledge anymore. They want results. **Be the one who gives it to them.**

What were your 3 key takeaways:

What 3 additional action steps are you going to take:

What is the deadline you're setting for each of these steps:

Chapter 21

The Future Of Social Media

I hope this book has not only taught you something about social media but has inspired you to take action. Even after two decades in this space, I still believe we're early. Platforms rise and fall, technology evolves, and yet one truth remains constant: **social media keeps reinventing how humans connect.**

I've watched every major shift of the last twenty-plus years. My-Space to Facebook. Facebook to Instagram. Instagram to TikTok. And now, AI is rewriting the rules all over again. Through it all, one thing has never changed: the creators who adapt win.

I do believe Web3 and decentralized social media will eventually have their moment. But I don't think we're there yet. The average person still faces too many technical barriers. Until that changes, I see a different, more immediate transformation unfolding, and it's exciting.

There are **two directions,** I believe will shape the future of social media:

1. From Phones to Wearables

It's no secret that Zuckerberg is pouring billions into wearable tech, from Oculus to Meta Ray-Bans. The latest models even project a display inside the lenses that only the wearer can see. That's going to completely change how we consume content.

For more than a decade, our phones have been the primary gateway to social media. But beyond faster chips and better cameras, there hasn't been much innovation in *how* we consume content. It's ripe for disruption.

As wearables become lighter, more powerful, and actually stylish, I believe they'll become the next major device for content consumption. Imagine a blend of augmented reality, live data overlays, and an AI assistant literally in your line of sight.

Yes, it sounds a little dystopian, but also revolutionary. I've used Meta Ray-Bans for over a year, and they've changed how quickly I can capture ideas and get information. I can easily see a future where creators design short, immersive formats specifically for glasses viewing, where your feed lives right in your vision.

2. The Rise of Real, Raw, Human Experiences

Despite my optimism for AI, I think people are exhausted and craving authenticity. Ironically, I believe AI will bring us *closer together* in person.

We're already seeing it: more conferences, meetups, and in-person communities forming because of connections made online.

When I hosted my first AI Marketing World conference, over 400 people showed up, people who'd first met me through social media.

Here's the paradox I've learned:

The more content gets automated, the more people crave genuine connection.The more AI fills our feeds, the more valuable authenticity becomes. The more we can do with technology, the more we need to remember what it means to be human.

And that's exactly why your **personal brand** matters now more than ever.

AI can write your scripts. It can edit your videos. It can schedule your posts. But it can't replicate **your story.** It can't duplicate **your perspective.** It can't replace **your humanity.**

Your humanity is your competitive advantage.

The creators who will thrive over the next five years aren't the ones with the most sophisticated AI tools. They're the ones who use those tools to amplify their authentic voice, not replace it. They're the ones who show up consistently, share vulnerably, and build *real* relationships with their audience.

After more than twenty years in this space, I can tell you one truth with absolute certainty: **your personal brand is the most important asset you can build.**

Not because of vanity. Not because of follower counts. But because your brand is the one thing that can't be automated, replicated, or taken away from you.

Platforms will come and go. Algorithms will change. But your voice, your story, your ability to connect with others on a human level, those will outlast every technological shift.

So yes, leverage AI. Automate the repetitive stuff. Streamline your workflow. But never lose sight of *why* people follow you: because you're real. Because you're relatable. Because when they see your content, they feel like they know you.

This is your moment. The barrier to entry has never been lower. The tools have never been more powerful. The opportunity has never been bigger.

But the one thing that will set you apart from the millions of other creators online isn't the technology you use. It's **you.**

Don't lose your humanity as you embrace technology. **Lean into it.** Let AI handle the busy work so you can focus on creating meaning. Use automation to make space for a deeper connection. Leverage these tools not to replace your voice, but to amplify it.

Because the future belongs to those who can blend the efficiency of technology with the irreplaceable power of human connection. The future belongs to those who build personal brands rooted in authenticity, expertise, and real value.

And if you're willing to show up and do the work, **the future belongs to you.**

So get out there. Create content. Build relationships. Go to conferences. Share your story. Use every tool at your disposal.

But most importantly, never forget that the most powerful asset you have isn't AI, editing software, or scheduling platforms. It's **you.**

Now go build something that matters.

What were your 3 key takeaways:

_____

_____

_____

What 3 additional action steps are you going to take:

_____

_____

_____

What is the deadline you're setting for each of these steps:

_____

_____

_____

AUSTIN ARMSTRONG

THE END

Gratitude

Thank you to my mom for all of your love and patience while raising me.

Special thank you to all of the Advanced Copy Readers: Dan Armstrong, Katie Brinkley, Jacqueline Crider, Donley Ferguson, Shanita Jones, Emma Rainville, and Dennis Yu

Thank you, again, to Dennis Yu for taking the time for writing the awesome forward.

Thank you to all of my mentors and pod team members.

Thank you to my editing team at SayThat Publishing.

Thank you to all of you who follow, comment, and like my content on social media, we're building a movement!

And BIG thank you to each of you who purchased and have read this book.

About Austin Armstrong

Austin Armstrong is a digital marketing strategist, two-time seven-figure entrepreneur, and global professional speaker known for turning complexity into clarity. With over two decades in online marketing, Austin has helped thousands of businesses and creators grow their brands, master short-form video, and harness the power of AI to scale their reach.

As the **Founder and CEO of Syllaby.io**, a leading AI platform for automated video creation and publishing, and **Co-Founder of AI Marketing World**, Austin has built an ecosystem at the forefront of the AI content revolution. His mission is simple: to provide the tips, tools, and strategies that have changed his life to help change yours, too.

Across platforms, Austin's content has reached **billions of views** and inspired a community of more than **four million followers** who trust his practical, down-to-earth approach to growth. His frameworks blend **authentic storytelling, smart systems, and data-driven creativity**, proving that viral success isn't luck; it's strategy.

A seasoned **keynote speaker and educator**, Austin has shared the stage with top innovators in marketing and technology and has taught **AI Entrepreneurship at Duke University**, equipping the next generation of creators and founders to use artificial intelligence for impact and innovation.

Through his work, Austin continues to champion one idea above all: **anyone can build influence and income online if they learn how to blend authenticity with automation.**

Connect with Austin

WEBSITES

www.AustinArmstrong.ai

www.Syllaby.io

https://aimarketingworld.co/

AUSTIN ARMSTRONG

SOCIAL MEDIA LINKS

www.facebook.com/Owwstin/

www.linkedin.com/in/austinarmstrong90/

www.tiktok.com/@usefulaiwebsites

www.youtube.com/@socialtypro

www.threads.com/@socialtypro

https://x.com/SocialtyPro

www.instagram.com/socialtypro

ADDITIONAL RESOURCES & DISCOUNT COUPONS

www.austinarmstrong.ai/resources

www.ingramcontent.com/pod-product-compliance
Lightning Source LLC
Chambersburg PA
CBHW071331210326
41597CB00015B/1413